Arab Dollars for Africa

First Published in 1976, the purpose of the book *Arab Dollars for Africa* is to indicate how Arab funds can be recycled into the African Economy. The long-term industrial future of the Arab oil producers is dependent on the availability of raw materials. Africa as a whole contains vast reserves of vital minerals, but they require considerable investment for their exploitation. The Arab states are well placed to participate in the development of the African economy both on the basis of state-to-state cooperation and through individual enterprises.

Africa and the Arab world share economic goals as members of the developing world and as key primary producers and have a common purpose in bringing about a new international economic order. This book deals in detail with investment opportunities in national development banks and in individual agricultural and industrial projects. This is an important historical analysis for scholars and researchers of African studies, international politics and geopolitics.

Arab Dollars for Africa

E. C. Chibwe

Routledge
Taylor & Francis Group

First published in 1976
by Croom Helm Ltd.

This edition first published in 2023 by Routledge
4 Park Square, Milton Park, Abingdon, Oxon, OX14 4RN

and by Routledge
605 Third Avenue, New York, NY 10017

Routledge is an imprint of the Taylor & Francis Group, an informa business

Publisher's Note
The publisher has gone to great lengths to ensure the quality of this reprint but points
out that some imperfections in the original copies may be apparent.

Disclaimer
The publisher has made every effort to trace copyright holders and welcomes
correspondence from those they have been unable to contact.

A Library of Congress record exists under ISBN: 085664174X

ISBN: 978-1-032-50344-8 (hbk)
ISBN: 978-1-003-39807-3 (ebk)
ISBN: 978-1-032-50345-5 (pbk)

Book DOI 10.4324/9781003398073

Arab Dollars for Africa

E.C. CHIBWE

CROOM HELM LONDON

First published 1976
© 1976 E.C. Chibwe

Croom Helm Ltd.
2-10 St. John's Road London SW11

ISBN 0-85664-174-X

Printed and bound in Great Britain by
REDWOOD BURN LIMITED
Trowbridge & Esher

Contents

TO MY CHILDREN

Chikwa, Chipampe and Lubala, hoping they shall live to see an affluent Africa in which poverty, ignorance and disease will all be things of the past.

Acknowledgements

The ideas and views expressed in this book represent, for the most part, some of my thoughts which I have cherished during the past ten years both as a student of economics and an administrator. These thoughts have been nurtured during the period I have served as Commissioner of Taxes and Permanent Secretary to the Zambian Treasury. They are personal and therefore do not reflect the thinking of the various institutions I have been privileged to serve.

The object of the exercise is twofold; to open a debate for those in the academic world and to open a dialogue between the policy makers of Arab and African states.

I wish to thank most sincerely all those people who assisted me in the course of writing this book. In particular I would like to express my special heartfelt thanks to H.E. the President Dr. K.D. Kaunda for writing a lucid foreword. I must also thank him for having afforded me the opportunity to work in the Zambian Treasury which enabled me to have a better understanding and appreciation of applied economics.

I wish to acknowledge with thanks the invaluable help I received from Mr. 'Tiny' Rowland. He allowed me to exploit his immense business knowledge of the African and the Arab world. He is one of the few western industrialists who can rightly claim to have participated in the economic development of several African countries. One Arab friend of mine said to me that there are few, if any, Arab kings or statesmen who do not count 'Tiny' Rowland as their personal friend. Mr. Rowland read my manuscripts and provided me with valuable comments.

Chapter 1 of this book represents a summary of about a hundred interviews I had with several of my Arab and Jewish friends. I found their accounts, arguments and judgement extremely rewarding. I acknowledge gratefully their assistance which, I am happy to record, was freely provided to me.

It would be remiss if I did not mention my two friends Bruce Munyama and Waza Kaunda who encouraged me to write this book and provided me with counsel throughout the course of my writing.

I owe a debt of gratitude to my wife who allowed me to desert my home now and again in order to obtain material for this book. My mother deserves special mention. It was she who encouraged me to go to school and at great personal sacrifice provided me with money for my secondary school education.

E.C. Chibwe

Foreword

The Arab oil producers announced a dramatic four hundred per cent increase in the price of crude oil in late 1973. This decision may well be regarded as a watershed in the history of the relationship between the developed countries and the Third World. It was the first major success scored by the producers of raw materials in the struggle for seeking just and remunerative prices for their scarce and exhaustible natural resources. By the time the tremors sent out by the decisions had died down, it had been established that the affluence and prosperity of the developed world is dependent in no small degree upon the raw material resources of the poorer countries. This realisation and the fact that the entire world came to accept the high prices and adjusted itself to the changed circumstances have also given hope to producers of other raw materials in developing countries for a similar improvement in the returns on their products as well.

Inevitably, the increased prices placed an additional burden on all countries. In view of the already severe constraints on financial resources in the developing countries, this additional burden has turned out to be very onerous indeed. Nevertheless, in the interest of higher principles and in the hope that a new international economic order based on the principles of fairness, justice and equity would ultimately prevail, the Third World has shown readiness to undertake this burden. One could legitimately expect in this context, however, our endeavour at seeking the new economic order would be supported, meaningfully and materially, by the oil producers. These countries, particularly in the Middle East, are now earning vast amounts of surplus financial resources. All of these surpluses cannot obviously be invested within their existing economic systems. This has given rise to the problems of recycling oil funds. There were hopeful signs, initially, that a fair proportion of these surpluses would be diverted to the poorer world. In the event, however, these countries have received only nominal amounts so far. In stark contrast, overwhelmingly large sums

7

have found their way back to the economies of the rich countries where quite often, these have been utilised for conspicuous consumption or at best, in acquiring equity in existing industrial establishments. Even in the best of circumstances, it would seem a great pity indeed if once again the resources of the developing countries were put to a use which would widen still further the gap between the 'haves' and the 'have-nots' of the world. There is, therefore, a strong case on economic, political and moral grounds that a much higher proportion of these surpluses should flow to poor countries where they can be utilised in creating much-required additional productive capacities.

Comrade Ephraim Chipampe Chibwe, who is currently Zambia's Ambassador to the Federal Republic of Germany and who has previously held high office in the Civil Service, has attempted an objective and in-depth analysis of these issues in this book. He has brought out the several facets of the situation and the problems which we in Africa face in this context. He has also attempted to indicate the directions in which solutions could be sought and found. Much diligent work has gone into the book. It covers a wide spectrum of Africa's economic commitments, ties and relations within the continent and with the rest of the world which have relevance to the recycling of oil funds. I am, therefore, happy to have said these few words by way of introduction to this thought-provoking book. I congratulate Comrade Chibwe for the praiseworthy effort. Even though these may not always be the same as those of the Government, I am impressed by the views expressed, the observations made and the various solutions suggested by Comrade Chibwe. I sincerely hope that these will receive attention and due consideration from all concerned and will provide the basis for fruitful cooperation between our Arab brothers and ourselves in Africa.

I am also happy to see a young civil servant having the right motivation, the initiative, capacity and perseverance to devote himself to an arduous task in spite of numerous official commitments and the limited time available to him. It is an encouraging example which is worthy of emulation by other comrades. Not only does it establish that there is no end to the pursuit of knowledge, but also that it is essential that we should share and disseminate our experience and knowledge to others and thus improve the quality of life in the society of which we are a part.

State House   His Excellency Dr Kenneth D. Kaunda
Lusaka   President

Introduction

The main purpose of this book is to pinpoint practical ways in which the surplus revenues accumulated by the Arab oil producing nations can be recycled into the African economy. I propose that Arab money be directed both into national development banks for purposes of general development and into individual agricultural or industrial projects. Thus the book deals in detail with what Arab investors (whether governments or private concerns) can expect from becoming involved in new African projects. Investors do not want to be passive; they are interested both in income and the execution of their projects. In this respect I suggest some particular concessions that African countries should consider making to the Arab investor in particular.

Quite apart from the financial commitments some Arab nations have made to help offset the often crippling oil price rises in the developing world, Arab investors have already shown a marked preference for being associated with individual projects in individual countries (usually those with a strong Islamic influence) rather than with unwieldy groups of countries. I suggest that this trend be both encouraged and extended beyond the confines of religious affiliations.

In the long term, the industrial future of the newly-rich Arab nations is tied up with the availability of raw materials. Africa as a whole contains vast reserves of vital minerals and can become a major agricultural producer. Naturally, investment opportunities vary from country to country, but history has shown that even the remote and poor parts of Africa can quickly become successful nations with a vital part to play in the world economic order.

Within the framework of state-to-state cooperation agreements I propose that the two parties form a council to implement the agreed objectives. Even where the Arab investor is not a government, the other party should be a government. Only in this way will the investor have cast-iron guarantees that the agreements can be reinforced and honoured.

In terms of technical expertise both the Arab and African nations are still developing, but participation in tendering for contracts should be on equal terms to citizens of the participant states. Thus before any project is put to international tender the two contracting parties should be satisfied that neither is competent enough to undertake any part of a project. The basic exceptions to the rule would be for purely technical reasons, i.e. to reduce transport costs or to ensure efficient management. Participation by a third party would thus be authorised in the larger-scale projects.

African reciprocation for Arab investment would include according preferential treatment to the Arab state or states in terms of imports and exports, and special tax concessions. As the Arab countries build up their industrial base they will need increasing quantities of African raw materials and in particular her minerals. This book therefore indicates a number of areas of possible Arab investment.

In tackling the technical aspects of Afro-Arab cooperation in development I also describe the broader political and economic issues that have brought the Third World to its present phase of demanding a new international economic order. It is significant that in the forums of the United Nations, the Organisation of African Unity and the Organisation of Petroleum Exporting Countries, it was the Algerian government that took the lead in proposing new international economic relationships — significant in that Algeria feels equally committed to the advancement of both Africa and the Arab world.

The old dominance of the industrial countries over the developing countries has begun to crumble in a remarkably short time. The process was accelerated when the Arabs unleashed their 'oil weapon' during the October 1973 Middle East War. However, it is important to realise that the oil price rises were not provoked entirely by motives of political gain in the Middle East alone, although the war provided the impetus. The price rises were rather the culmination of years of poorly coordinated attempts to show the industrial nations that the era of economic exploitation was over. The lead in forcing up prices was taken by Iran, a country which has no political axe to grind in the Middle East and refused to take part in oil boycotts, whether of the US and Holland or of South Africa.

One Middle East expert has observed that the use of the oil weapon in 1973 was an attempt to put history back on its right course. It proved that the Western countries could not function without oil and that soon they would have to allow other nations to join their exclusive 'club', with its high standards of living, education, social welfare, etc. For this reason the Arabs' successes have given them profound satisfaction. For them, history is now pointing in the right direction.

But what of Africa and the rest of the Third World? The developing nations have suffered economic, and in some cases, political disruption as a result of the oil price rises and they are now desperately searching for both short-term and long-term solutions to their difficulties. But the picture is not entirely hopeless. The events of the past year have shown that Africa too is gaining confidence in asserting its right to fair treatment in trading arrangements and commodity prices. Early in 1975 the countries of Africa, the Caribbean and the Pacific (ACP) negotiated more favourable trading arrangements with the European Economic Community (EEC) than had ever prevailed before. The details of the Lome Convention that resulted from these negotiations are dealt with at length at the end of this book.

Since African countries began to gain their independence in the late 1950s, the continent's international relationships have been dominated by economic dependence on the West and exploring avenues of cooperation with the East, but the Arab actions of 1973 have introduced a new area of special relationships. Not only does part of the Arab world belong to Africa and the Organisation of African Unity (OAU) but all Arab countries belong, like Africa, to the Third World and non-aligned groupings. There is therefore a built-in solidarity of interests.

Despite this solidarity most of black Africa has also been on good terms with Israel, which made strenuous efforts to provide technical, military and financial aid all over the continent. Now this relationship has come to an abrupt end. From the moment on 16 October 1973 when Israeli forces crossed the Suez Canal to invade Egypt (an OAU founding member), Africa's diplomatic relationships with Israel were irrevocably severed.

To give a broad perspective to my study of what the Arab nations should now be doing to help Africa in its present economic plight I start with a brief but hopefully objective analysis of the Middle East conflict, its momentous world-wide effects and Africa's reactions. I hope my contribution will help to clear away some of the misunderstandings that still impede the arrival of a new international economic order.

1

The Middle East Conflict

When the Six Day War broke out in 1967 between Israel and its Arab neighbours the news was received in various parts of the world with mixed feelings. Some people believed it to be a religious war between Moslems and Jews. Others maintained that the war was politically motivated — a confrontation between the two big superpowers, the US and the USSR. A third school of thought maintained that for Israel it was a war of survival and for the Arabs a battle to end Israel's expansionist policy. As with the current war in Northern Ireland there was no consensus of opinion as to the causes, motives and effects.

If the Israelis and the Arabs fell under the category of 'religious fanatics' then no doubt the war would have started without proper preparation and each side would have expected fate to take its course. But this was not the case in 1967, and even less so in 1973. The conflict was systematically planned and systematically fought. Little was left to chance or fate.

I prefer to see the Middle East conflict as revenge of the twentieth century upon the nineteenth century, or in other words a war of the Third World against the industrialised world and all its manifestations. The industrialised countries were the first to introduce mechanisation, but their mechanical monsters have needed ever more feeding with raw materials — hence the imperial expansion into Asia and Africa in the nineteenth century. Europe's great 'scramble for Africa' in the 1880s was undertaken for the acquisition of raw materials. It was often simply a question of staking a claim, so that the other 'scramblers' should not get it, whatever it was. There was no thought for the local inhabitants and often no idea of what actual resources each territory possessed. Every nation merely made sure that the other nations did not trespass on its claims.

As for the Middle East, each European power had its 'sphere of influence'. The so-called 'fertile crescent', extending from

Iraq to Morocco around the southern shores of the Mediterranean, was divided between Britain (Egypt, Palestine and Transjordan), France (Algeria, Morocco, Tunisia, Syria and Lebanon) and Italy (Libya). The Mediterranean was seen as a securely European lake, until the voice of Arab nationalism was first heard in the 1930s and 1940s.

By one of history's great coincidences, Arab nationalism developed simultaneously with the discovery of oil in the Middle East. But few people realised the significance of the connection. At the outset oil was cheap energy. Once you hit it the oil went on spurting out of the ground until the well was dry. By contrast coal was an expensive and dangerous commodity to produce, and so while the European nations were slowly but irrevocably closing down their coal mines and consuming ever more oil the nationalist movements of the Third World were gathering strength, to the point where they could drastically upset the balance of industrial power. The Third World was also rapidly learning how to use the industrial world's machines. All these factors started a process that led inexorably to the present situation, in which the peoples of Africa, the Middle East, Asia and Latin America no longer want to be exploited just to feed the machinery of the industrial nations.

As the young countries of the world have gained in national pride, their development has given them a new identity, a new society and a new culture, in many cases a combination of the best of the old and the new worlds (though in other countries people have reason to think that they are getting the worst of both worlds). The Arab nations have been very much preoccupied with new ideas of development, but at the same time they have adhered to their predominant religion and culture. The Arabs are, however, unique in the Third World in that they find themselves sitting on two-thirds of the world's known oil reserves — hence their unprecedented power at this crucial period of world history.

The thorn in the Arabs' side is the state of Israel — an unusual phenomenon by any standards, but one that the Arabs interpret both as the expiation of Europe's guilt for 2,000 years of persecution of the Jews and as an inhuman experiment that has deprived the Palestinians of their homeland. Many also regard Israel as the West's economic bridgehead in the Middle

East — designed to divide and recolonise the entire region.

The Jews

For 2,000 years the Jews were persecuted wherever they lived. They were usually forced to live in closed communities so they could be easily identified and used as scapegoats when rulers wanted to divert political or economic crises. Wholesale expulsion or slaughter of Jewish communities has been a regular occurrence in the history of these unfortunate people.

By all the historical precedents, once the Jews lost their Palestinian homeland and were dispersed throughout the western world they should also have lost their identity, like other conquered peoples. But the Jews did not. They became the shuttlecocks of Europe whom no-one would accept. Their only security lay in their common identity and suffering, their traditions and their religion. Such wealth as they made had to be transportable, either in the form of academic knowledge or jewellery and other light valuables.

The pattern continued until the nineteenth century, when the industrial revolution and concomitant social changes brought new hope to the Jewish communities. Zionism was born. In the face of unrelenting persecution Jewish idealists came forward with a new idea : no-one wants us so let us try to regain our self-respect, let us become a nation again; for that we need land — the land we lost by conquest and which is ours by heritage.

Every Jew has Palestine built into his religion. When they celebrate Passover, Jews toast: 'Next year in Jerusalem.' But the greatest exponent of Zionism, Theodor Herzl, identified one of the problems of his Utopia when he remarked that no nation can be composed entirely of bankers and academics (as the Jews had almost exclusively become through centuries of exile). Herzl wanted people to work with their hands and to go back to the land. His ideas came at the right time for the young, often unemployed, Jewish youths of central and eastern Europe at the turn of the century. They emigrated to Palestine in small groups, with no money or prospects, only a burning faith to build a new land.

The pioneering ideology of the early Zionists brought about the highly successful Kibbutz system and made the desert bloom. It combined the positive aspects of modern technology with the maintenance of traditional social values, but as with all pioneering societies there was an immediate 'apartness' from the resident people who had been tilling the land in their own undisturbed way for centuries. The immigrants bought land and developed it at a furious pace, always with the thought that a high standard of living would have to be maintained if more immigrants were to come. Land and wealth were accumulated. But so was the resentment of the Palestinian Arabs.

The British had a mandate over Palestine and after the First World War the Balfour Declaration promised Palestine to the Jews as their homeland. But the British were also well aware of the growing Arab nationalism of the Middle East and were careful not to inflame the situation, so they prevaricated. A British proposal in 1937 that Palestine should be partitioned into an Arab and a Jewish state was rejected by the Arabs. Another proposal in 1939 that an independent state be set up after a ten-year period of limited Jewish immigration was rejected on both sides. Because the British seemed unwilling to honour the Balfour Declaration in full, Jews began to form underground armies and many became guerrillas.

After the Second World War the incredible truth about the Nazi death camps became known. The sympathies aroused by Hitler's attempt to exterminate European Jewry combined with the pressures of Zionism in the US to produce a UN scheme for partitioning Palestine. Half of Jerusalem became Jewish and a small part of the land was given to the Jews. The boundaries were artificial and difficult to maintain and so Israel was born in war, and has remained at war. Since Israel became a member of the UN in 1949 the Middle East has become a war arsenal.

The Arabs argue about Israel: the West is guilty and feels guilty for its centuries of anti-semitism; the hand of the West has been behind Israel's expansionist moves in 1948, 1956 and 1967. Israel's economic progress is phony; considering the aid that has poured in from the US, its citizens should be massively wealthy, but instead of wealth there has been only spending on arms and armed aggression.

On the other hand, the Jews argue that the Arabs never tilled the land of Palestine, they neglected it; the Arabs were not sent away by the Jews but were told to go by the other Arab nations so as to await a triumphant return; the land allocated to the Jews originally was indefensible and so land captured in battle is essential for Israel's security; the Arabs are jealous of Israel's tremendous economic advances.

It has been said that only the Arabs and the Jews can find a solution to the Middle East problem, but the roots of the dispute lie somewhere outside the Middle East. Any meaningful conference to settle the problems posed by Israel's existence should include not only Arabs and Jews but also the two superpowers, the US and the USSR, both of whom are directly interested in the dispute.

The Arabs

An Arab can be defined as one whose identity is bound to the Arab world as a whole, in terms of language, culture and religion. An Arab may be descended from Kurdish, Armenian, Negro or Berber stock, but if the central facts of history are the mission of Mohammed and the memory of the Arab empire, and if he cherishes the language and its cultural heritage, then he is a true Arab.

The Islamic religion is often identified with the Arabs because it was the religion which for the first time in their history was to give them courage and determination to conquer other races and acquire new dominions. According to the Arabs, the spirit of Mohammed was always the driving force in the conquest. Many scholars have said that 'without the Koran the Arabs would have neither arts and humanities nor law'.

In pursuance of the objective put forward by Mohammed, after his death his followers successfully conquered great parts of Europe, Africa and Asia. They were following the footsteps of the Romans who had also, centuries earlier, ruled part of Africa, Asia and Europe. The new Arab empire stretched from Central Asia through the Middle East and North Africa to the Atlantic Ocean. The year 655 AD marks their greatest victory when they conquered the Byzantines. John Laffin has observed:

Arabic civilisation grew rich and diverse and the Arab sense of heritage and tradition became as perceptual as it had earlier been merely conceptual. In many areas it did not interfere with the internal civil and religious administration of the conquered peoples. This enlightened control was particularly welcome to those who had been subject to much harsher Byzantine masters. Even the Christian population of Egypt and Syria, while detesting Islam, preferred its rule to that of the Byzantines.

Because of the animosity of Christians the Arabs were unable to extend their trade and influence to much of Western Europe. Despite this handicap their trade reached Norway, England and Baltic lands through the middlemen who smuggled Arab wealth and traded it in areas which were not under Arab influence. In 831 AD the Arabs occupied Sicily but were unable to capture Naples and Italy, although they succeeded in making the Pope pay respect to the Islamic religion. The Arabs were concerned about the welfare of the people they conquered. In Sicily they introduced new methods of agriculture. They irrigated the land on an extensive scale and were able to produce more food for the inhabitants. As a result of improved methods, the land was able to yield more crops per acre and was able to accommodate imported plants such as oranges, date palms and sugar cane from other lands.

Spain, which was first occupied by the Arabs in 810 AD, derived many benefits from their rule. Previously the nobles and the Roman clergy had dominated not only the political but also the economic life of the Spaniards. They jointly owned land which was cultivated by the peasants for little or no pay. When the Arabs took over the reins of government, they introduced sweeping land reforms and land was distributed to the peasants. The Arabs can rightly lay claim to the introduction of socialism for the first time in the history of Spain!

There is no denying the benefits that Arabic and Islamic civilisation brought to Europe. In Spain, the Arabs set up institutions of higher learning which attracted scholars from all over Europe. Treasured Greek literature reached Europe through Arabic translations and yet today one finds few modern scholars who recognise the Arab contribution to science and philosophy. If it were not for Arab advances in mathematics in particular, 'Western technology' would not have evolved as fast as it did. When Europe was stagnant under the Dark Ages, Arabic literature, philosophy, mathematics and medicine were flourishing.

Some modern commentators think that Arab unity can only express itself in the negative, in a desire to eliminate the Jews. But in the past Arab unity was always expressed positively and there is no reason to think that it will not be expressed positively again. In the Middle Ages the Arabs united their empire under a strong culture and a powerful religion, despite the racial and geographical differences in the subject territories.

Early Arab greatness was, however, eclipsed by the rise of Europe. The Arab world began to fragment and to succumb to foreign conquest until by the nineteenth century the Mediterranean was a completely European sea. The Arab star only began to rise again in the 1940s, simultaneously with the creation of the State of Israel. The weak Arab response to the challenge posed by Israel was to goad young nationalists into more positive action against foreign interference in the Middle East. The foremost and most charismatic of these nationalists was Egypt's Colonel Abdul Gamal Nasser.

Nasser's interpretation of the creation of Israel in 1948 was as follows:

The world imperialist forces and monopolies aim at fixed goals, namely to put the Arab territory extending from the Ocean to the Gulf under their military control, in order to be able to continue exploitation and loot its wealth. Imperialistic intrigues have gone to the extent of seizing a part of Arab territory of Palestine, in the heart of Arab motherland, and usurping it without any justification of right or law, the aim being to establish a military Fascist regime which cannot live except by military threats. The real danger of these threats emanates from the fact that Israel is the tool of imperialism. At the present, the United Arab Republic is, both historically and actually, the only Arab nation which can assume the responsibility of building a national army capable of deterring the Zionist imperialist aggressive plans.

The Arabs believe that the Arab-Israel conflict is not between the Arabs and Jews, but between the Arabs and imperialists. Israel is nothing more than a scapegoat. The history of the war supports this view. Nasser had this to say: 'Our Arab countries have not ceased for centuries to be the goal of imperialists' attacks and enmity, as if imperialism wanted to avenge an ancient wrong on the nation that brought civilisation to their countries with the conquest of Caliphate after Mohammed.'

On 20 March 1958, Nasser said: 'It was England and France that attacked this region under the name of the crusades, and the crusades were nothing else but British-French imperialism.' He believed that the main purpose of imperialism was:

> To degrade us and acquire what was in our hands and under our feet, to exploit our wealth and our markets for its own benefit, to take our land as a base for its armies, so that they should consume the fruits of our land in peace and destroy our buildings with their own hands or by the hands of their enemies, after which they would sow the seeds of corruption and dissension among us, liquidate the foundations of our nationality and muzzle us to prevent our recalling the grandeur of our past, deaden our hearts to make us insensible of our glorious achievement and steal away our minds and this world of ours.

Chapter 10 of the Egyptian National Charter makes it clear beyond any reasonable doubt that the Arabs in the Middle East are fighting against imperialism and not Israel. It states in part: 'The insistence of the people on liquidating the Israeli aggression on a part of Palestine land is a determination to liquidate one of the most dangerous pockets of imperialist resistance against the struggle of peoples.'

Since the October 1973 War things have begun to go the right way for the Arabs, to the point that Nasser's successor, President Sadat, was able to say on 1 June 1975: 'There is no other problem which is easier to solve than the Middle East problem.' The fact that he was saying this at a summit conference with President Ford of the US (in Salzburg) reflects his supreme confidence in the new situation.

In a lunch-time toast on the same occasion Sadat was able to spell out the Arabs' terms and for the first time there was a chance that America might be prepared to listen:

Belligerency can be terminated and peace can reign all over the Middle East, only when all the countries involved, including the superpowers, adhere to the recognition of independence, and territorial integrity of states, the inadmissability of acquisition of territory by force, the acceptance and basic kind of self-determination for the Palestinian people and their right to live in their own homes.

On the economic front too the Arabs have found new confidence. Their decision to increase the price of oil was paying handsome dividends. By their dramatic action, the Arabs entered the life of each and every individual both in the developed and developing countries.

Experts have observed that history will see the oil war of 1973 as an attempt to make history turn right. The oil war proved beyond any reasonable doubt that the western countries could not function without it. For the first time in the living memory of the Western countries of Europe and America, the oil weapon, and not atomic energy or any other nuclear weapon, was bringing the unconquerable industrial countries to their knees. John Laffin, speaking about the Arab successes in 1973, said: 'This gave profound satisfaction to Arabs from the Arabian Gulf to the Atlantic, for it wiped away some of the shame of centuries of humiliation. History was now pointing in the right direction.' In 1974, there was a consensus of opinion among economists that the survival of Europe was dependent upon the financial assistance the continent received from the Middle East. In the short run, for most countries of Europe to survive, they had to rely on the temporary recycling of Arab dollars in Europe, which in plain language meant borrowing from Arab countries on a short-term basis. The long-term solution lay in Europe increasing the volume of trade with the countries of the Middle East. The only way to pay for Arab oil was by selling more goods and services to the Arab oil exporting nations.

Foreign involvement

The involvement of the two superpowers in the Middle East deserves critical observation. Smaller mortals at the UN have charged that without the support of the two superpowers the war would have been concluded a long time ago. If it is true that the superpowers were responsible for the conflict in the Middle East, what benefits are likely to accrue to them? This is a fundamental question which is always being asked by those who genuinely want to see peace in that troubled spot of the world. One diplomat accredited to the Federal Republic of Germany ironically said: 'There is nothing special about the Middle East. It is just one of the testing grounds for the new improved defensive and offensive missiles of the superpowers.' This is a superficial answer given to a vital and serious question, but it possibly contains some truth.

It is generally believed that whoever controls the Mediterranean Sea will have direct access to the Indian Ocean. The superpowers hold the view that since the Indian Ocean is bounded by the continent of Africa and the sub-continent of India, both of which are militarily impotent, the Indian Ocean is open to military competition. The Mediterranean area itself attracts a lot of attention from the superpowers. It is bounded to the north by members of the European Economic Community, and both economically and politically, the EEC has become a force to reckon with. Any peaceful *détente* between the superpowers without the participation of Europe is meaningless. The NATO countries believe that the Soviet Union is working for the disintegration of Europe and wants a power vacuum there so that she can move in, control Europe and turn it into a Communist state. As long as the American forces remain in Europe and the Mediterranean, NATO believes that the Soviet Union will neither strike nor cause any trouble.

To the south and east of the Mediterranean are rich Arab oil producing countries. Their potential wealth has been a considerable attraction to the two superpowers and their collaborators. When war broke out in the Middle East in October 1973 European countries began to question, for the first time, their undivided support for Israel. Traditionally, NATO countries have been pro-Israel but the business community was beginning to appreciate the necessity of remaining on the best possible terms with the Arabs.

The Arabs rediscovered their strength in the realisation that oil is the world's major source of energy, and provides the key to scientific, political, military and economic power. The events in Europe prove beyond any reasonable doubt that the Arab oil weapon is strong enough to make the world tremble.

One European diplomat in Bonn said that the influence of Western Europe in the Middle East conflict was zero. Other things being equal, Western Europe would support Israel, but unfortunately for the Europeans things were not equal. Europe needed oil and Israel had no oil to offer them. For reasons of survival they elected to support the Arabs.

Some people have raised the possibility that if the Arabs continued to use oil as a weapon to intimidate the international community the United States might decide to seize the oil militarily. In that event, the European countries would play an important role. They would either allow or deny bases to American planes. On condition that the Americans promised to share oil with her NATO allies she would have no problem in obtaining landing rights.

The chances of the US directly attacking the Arabs now appear remote. Dr Kissinger's statements about the need for peace in the Middle East have given the impression that the United States is genuinely seeking for a solution to the Middle East crisis and is prepared to force Israel to make concessions to the Arabs in return for increased US involvement in their economic development (Egypt's new westernisation is a case in point). Current indications are that the United States is endeavouring to find a solution which will provide for coexistence among the states of the region.

HE Dr Kenneth David Kaunda
President of the Republic of Zambia

HM King Khaled bin Abdul-Aziz bin Abdurrahman al Saud of
Saudi Arabia

2

African Diplomacy in the Middle East

In 1973 Israel's diplomacy not only suffered a setback in Europe but was completely disrupted in Africa. Nearly all the member-states of the Organisation of African Unity (OAU) who had formerly had diplomatic links with Israel broke off their relations between September and November. Togo started the ball rolling on 21 September 1973, and was followed by Zaire on 4 October. After the fighting broke out on 6 October the following countries broke their relations with Israel in this order: Rwanda, Dahomey, Mauritania, Upper Volta, Cameroon, Equatorial Guinea, Tanzania, Madagascar, Central African Republic, Ethiopia, Nigeria, Zambia, Gambia, Senegal, Ghana, Gabon, Sierra Leone, Kenya, Liberia and Ivory Coast. Botswana was one of the last, announcing its decision on 13 November.

The psychological breaking point was the Israeli advance into Egypt on 16 October — an invasion of African soil that OAU states could not forgive. Yet despite the apparent suddenness of the break with Israel there had been considerable diplomatic manoeuvring in the early part of 1973 — a year that was in fact unusual in OAU history in that there was unprecedented cohesion between African states, not only on the Middle East, but also in relations with Europe. Contrary to many predictions, agreement was reached for a continental approach to negotiations with the EEC. These negotiations led to the Lome agreement of February 1975.

The extent of the break with Israel was surprising when one considers that many countries had been very close to the Jewish state, but despite considerable Israeli business interests and the extent of Israeli aid, the risks of not siding with the Arabs were too great even for those countries most favourably disposed to Israel — Ethiopia, Ghana, Ivory Coast, Kenya, Zaire and Zambia. Looking back it is perhaps difficult to see that Africa's desertion of Israel was not motivated by fear of the Arabs' 'oil weapon'. In fact the oil issue was irrelevant at that stage. The punitive nature of oil sanctions did not become manifest for some weeks after the African nations had already acted. The causes lay in behind-the-scenes diplomatic manoeuvring during the early 1970s. Ever since the foundation of the OAU in 1963, the Arab states had been applying steady pressure on Black Africa to come round to their point of view on Israel. But equally strong was the attraction of Israeli assistance. So for the whole of the 1960s the Arabs and Africans agreed to differ. Even in the 1967 Six Day War only one Black African country (Guinea) broke with Israel.

In 1971 the OAU's outwardly 'neutral' position enabled the appointment of ten African heads of state as mediators in the Middle East, and Africa for the first time played an active and significant role in the diplomacy of the area. The 'Ten Wise Men' failed, as many had done before them, but they were at least able to talk on consecutive days with Egyptian and Israeli leaders, something that even Dr Kissinger had difficulty in doing in 1973.

The failure of the OAU's mission was blamed on Israel's blank refusal to negotiate about withdrawal from captured Arab territory, and this refusal brought Africa several degrees closer to the Arab position. The OAU summit at Rabat revealed new African militancy in the passing of a tough anti-Israel resolution. In 1973 the trend continued; Libya's Colonel Gaddafy was even sufficiently encouraged by Africa's new stance to suggest that the Addis Ababa summit of the OAU be moved to Cairo unless Ethiopia broke its relations with Israel. Compromise prevailed on that occasion, but the affair made Emperor Haile Selassie aware of the difficulty of keeping the OAU headquarters in Addis, while his country remained on good terms with Tel Aviv.

Meanwhile Israel was blindly confident of keeping good relations with Black Africa. In August 1973, the Israeli Foreign Minister, Abba Eban, said that Israel hoped to maintain and enlarge its diplomatic presence. But already the die was cast. Uganda, Chad, and the Congo Republic had broken relations in 1972, followed in early 1973 by Niger, Mali and Burundi.

September 1973 was the occasion of the Non-Aligned

Conference in Algiers. The Arab states succeeded in getting resolutions passed pledging full support for Egypt, Syria and Jordan in recovering their lost territories and calling on all member-states to 'work on a diplomatic, economic, military and cultural boycott of Israel'. Togo and Zaire were the first to follow this advice. Zaire's General Mobutu Sese Seko announced his break at the UN on 4 October in a most dramatic manner, saying that faced with a choice between a friend (Israel) and a brother (the Arab world) he had no option but to choose a brother. Israel was most upset as it had, up to then, been contributing to training Zaire's military forces.

Then came the war on 6 October. Some African heads of state, such as Nigeria's General Gowon, remained reluctant to cut off contact with the Israelis, and wanted to maintain the OAU's neutrality. But whatever the outcome of the military battle, the Arabs had won the diplomatic war.

An extraordinary session of the OAU Council of Ministers was held in Addis Ababa on 19-21 November 1973. For the first time, resolutions were passed equating Zionism in Israel with apartheid in South Africa. The Africans pressed the Arabs to include South Africa in their list of unfriendly nations who should suffer an oil boycott. The Arab summit in Algiers that followed shortly afterwards agreed to ban Arab oil exports to the white-ruled South and to set up technical and financial aid to Black Africa.

But in this unprecedented solidarity between African and Arab were the seeds of disagreement. Major Kwame Baah, Ghana's Foreign Minister, told the OAU Council of Ministers that the Arab oil-producers would have to take account of the special needs of the developing sub-Saharan countries and that the African states had no way of insulating their economies against the effects of the oil price increases. An editorial in *Africa* magazine crystallised much that was being said all over the continent:

> Hopefully we are witnessing the beginning of an era of cooperation between the Arab world and Africa south of the Sahara. This could lead, if properly orientated, to a new partnership between the Middle East and Black Africa. There are evidently important obstacles that stand in the

way of sustained Afro-Arab solidarity. Black Africa and the Arab world are linked by territory, but in spite of the common tie through the Moslem religion, they remain separated by many historical and psychological factors. Memories of Arab slave hunts are a painful reminder of the erstwhile relationship between the Blacks and the Arabs of the African continent . . . Our dealings, to bear the right fruit, must be organised on a proper basis. Today one group negotiates as a powerful block while the members of the other react to the stimulus of that block as separate satellites. This was shown in the disgraceful, disorganised manner in which distraught African states bowed their heads one by one to concerted Arab pressure . . .

3
Effects of Oil Price Increases in Africa

Arabs had for a long time believed that the countries of Western Europe and North America were on the side of Israel. They also believed that these countries would influence Israel to withdraw from the Arab occupied territory and so in October 1973 the Arabs decided to use oil as a political weapon. They would reduce oil output by 5 per cent every month until their demands were met. Their next step was to ban oil exports to the US and the Netherlands. These bans, however, were soon found to be ineffective and were lifted during 1974. Also in October 1973, the countries of the Organisation of Petroleum Exporting Countries (OPEC) increased the posted price of oil from 3.02 dollars per barrel to 5.11 dollars per barrel. In December 1973, the posted price was fixed at 11.651 dollars per barrel.

The industrial countries of Europe, America and Japan reacted in different ways. Production in certain sectors fell, not necessarily due to a lack of oil but due to a lack of consumer demand. Car sales fell drastically. Production in oil consuming industries had to be cut back. Many countries introduced oil saving measures and temporary petrol rationing.

The effects on the West were certainly serious and still have not been fully calculated or compensated for, but when all things are taken into account one finds that the developing countries suffered more than the industrial world. For developed countries the increase in the price of oil simply meant a change in their terms of trade. It was an increase in the indebtedness to the oil producing countries who were claiming a larger share of their national income. The developed countries were able to stand this temporary disequilibrium because for most of them the oil price increase would be paid for through their gold holdings held as monetary reserves. The oil producing countries have not yet established their money markets and therefore the Arab money will filter back into the monetary systems of these countries and will thus offset the current account deficit. The industrial countries can correct the disequilibrium by increasing the price of their export goods to developing countries, i.e. when the Arabs increased the price of oil Japan decided to increase export receipts by 23 per cent by increasing the volume by only 5 per cent.

On the contrary developing countries cannot rely on a more or less automatic inflow to offset the deficits. As we have pointed out, the industrial countries will have to correct the imbalance by increasing the price of exports to developing countries but the developing countries cannot balance their accounts by increasing their exports of raw materials. Some of these countries have to borrow money in order to buy consumer goods to feed their huge population. They have overstretched their ability to borrow; they already have heavy debt burdens. To most of them the increase in the price of oil demands that they reduce the imports of other capital goods, which in turn will affect their development efforts. As poor countries they cannot improve on their purchasing power by borrowing from abroad.

For its part the Paris-based Organisation for Economic Cooperation and Development (OECD) has written of the oil price rises that 'many of the countries which are hardest hit are at the same time those which, for reasons of their low *per capita* income and general intractability of their development problems, are least able to carry the burden'. The 1974 report of the OECD's Development Assistance Committee said that the total increase in the developing countries' oil import bill was roughly 10,000 million dollars in 1974 alone. A typically badly hit country is Ethiopia, whose 1974 oil bill added 20 per cent to the cost of her imports compared with 1973. Uganda had an increase estimated at 15 per cent.

Most of Africa comes under the category the OECD calls 'poor countries with limited resilience and with large sectors of the population living close to subsistence, where even small increases in the oil bill may constitute an onerous burden and cause serious disruption'. Experts working for the UN Economic Commission for Africa (ECA) Natural Resources Division estimated that in 1974 the thirty African non-oil-producing countries spent 1,250 million dollars on oil imports alone, even if they consumed no more than in 1973, when their oil imports had cost 470 million dollars. This addition of some 780 million dollars for the higher petroleum costs was estimated to have raised their total import bill in 1974 to about 8,400 million dollars, 'and this at a time when essential foodstuffs and other imports were increasing in price at a fairly rapid rate'. The net result would be 'a restriction in consumption generally, and finally a slow-down of the countries' economic expansion'. The ECA experts went on to list Africa's other woes: increased costs of thermal electric production and transport, costs that are passed on to the consumers; increased shipping costs; increased fertiliser costs with adverse effects on crop production; and higher air travel costs that hit the tourist industry.

The initial reduction in oil supplies badly affected the thirteen countries that have their own oil refineries almost as much as the seventeen which have no refineries. The activities of the refineries were restricted and the countries without refineries found during the crisis period that products intended for them were delivered to other customers.

Africa's energy needs

It is true that most African countries need oil energy exclusively for commercial purposes, while their domestic demands such as cooking and heating are met by the use of animal dung or wood. Unlike the industrial countries whose domestic needs are satisfied by oil, coal and hydro-electric energy, most African countries use these forms of energy for exclusively commercial purposes.

The present exploration results have indicated that Africa south of the Sahara is not rich in crude oil. In 1974, Africa south of the Sahara had only four net exporters of oil: Nigeria, Zaire, Gabon and Congo. Nigeria has been a member of OPEC since 1971 and Gabon became an associate member in 1973. Exploration for crude oil has taken place in Zambia, Tanzania, Kenya, Ethiopia, Somalia, Sudan, Chad, Niger, Mali, Mauritania, Ghana and Sierra Leone, but the results have been disappointing.

In the absence of oil, African countries have looked for other forms of energy. Coal deposits have been found and opened up in some African countries. Coal is used both for commercial and non-commercial purposes. It is generally consumed in the producer country. The current producers are Zambia, Nigeria, Zaire and Swaziland. The exploitable reserves in this area amount to 500 million tons distributed as follows: Zambia, 115 million tons; Nigeria, 350 million tons; Zaire, 73 million.

For many African countries hydro-electric energy is the main source for production of electricity. This form of electrical energy is cheaper to produce and maintain. Once you have incurred the initial capital expenditure you will have little expenditure to incur for maintenance purposes. But this form of energy has a major disadvantage in that energy produced from water power can only be transmitted within a given distance, and often at great expense over high tension lines. In 1974 the main large hydro-electric power stations were Kafue and Kariba in Zambia, Inga in Zaire, Kainji in Nigeria and Akosombo in Ghana.

The escalating increases in oil prices in 1974 have caused economic chaos in most African countries. Except for Nigeria, Gabon, Zaire and the Congo, the rest of the independent countries south of the Sahara have experienced trade deficits in relation to their trade with the oil producing countries. Kenya, Tanzania and Mali have used up all their foreign exchange reserves. In 1975 if they have to buy additional supplies of crude oil the international community will have to come to their rescue.

From 1961 to 1970 oil prices were stable. The prices were not static but the increases were within a reasonable margin: they were not sharp enough to disrupt the terms of trade between the oil exporting countries and the oil importing countries. Suddenly in 1973 the prices were more than doubled. Even countries like the United States, which is supposed to be a self-sufficient consumer society, were caught unaware. By December 1974, the price of crude oil was more than quadrupled. In 1970 the price of crude oil was 2 dollars per barrel (14 dollars per ton); by the end of 1974 the price of crude oil was 12 dollars per barrel (84 dollars per ton).

The oil producing countries of OPEC have argued that since the prices of capital and consumer goods from the industrial countries in 1972 were five to six times more than they were in

1960, in order to be in equilibrium as far as trade with the industrial countries is concerned they had to increase the price of crude oil. To achieve this they increased taxes on royalties and profits earned by multinational companies operating in their territories.

The effect of this decision has been a flow of foreign exchange from the oil importing countries to the OPEC members. In 1970 the OPEC countries earned 7,800 million dollars. In 1974 they netted 100,000 million dollars. It is this accumulated surplus which has created economic and monetary disturbance in the international community. The propensity to spend of OPEC countries is limited by their capacity to consume and hence their capital must find outlets in both the industrial and the developing countries of the world, particularly Africa, where one finds that in the late twentieth century there is still abject poverty.

For the countries of Africa the increase in the price of oil resulted in a colossal increase in the oil bill and a corresponding reduction in the output of their raw materials and finished goods. Oil energy is used by practically all major industries and therefore any increase in the price of oil will substantially affect the running costs of such industries.

The agricultural sector is predominant in most developing countries. Petro-chemicals are essential ingredients in the production of fertilisers and therefore the escalating price of crude oil has had adverse effects on the agricultural sector. These developing countries have been forced to choose between alternative evils. With their limited financial resources they were forced by circumstances either to reduce their output or maintain their output in the agricultural sector and abandon some of their essential projects in their development plans. The World Bank estimated that in order to maintain moderate growth rates the developing countries would need financial aid of the magnitude of 6,800 million dollars for 1975, and between 10,000 and 12,000 million dollars between 1975 and 1980.

It has been asserted that African countries can absorb the shock of the increase in the price of oil because the prices of their raw materials have gone up. On the contrary, the price of most raw materials from Africa has gone down. In 1974 within a period of ten months the price of copper dropped from £900 per metric ton to £544 per metric ton. For Zambia and Zaire this meant a reduction of almost 50 per cent in their estimated revenue. Other African countries are in an even worse position. They have utilised the bulk of their foreign exchange and therefore they no longer have sufficient cash to pay for additional increases in the price of oil. These countries include Tanzania, Ghana, Ethiopia, Somalia, Kenya, Madagascar and Sudan. Some of them are so poor that their gross national product per head per year is no more than 200 dollars.

The effect on some oil importing countries of Africa has baffled most African economists. It is generally believed that any increase in imported commodities should adversely affect consumer countries who are far away from the port of entry. The recent price increases in crude oil seem to have disproved this axiom. In the case of countries which have the advantage of bordering an ocean, the increase in the f.o.b. prices of crude oil has affected a larger amount of the c.i.f. price of their imports than those countries which are in the hinterland. If one takes Zambia and Tanzania as typical examples one discovers that the quadruple increase in the price of crude oil has had a more adverse effect on Tanzania than on Zambia. The quadruple increase in the f.o.b. prices for crude oil amounts to a rise of about 100 per cent in the c.i.f. prices of refinery products. For Zambia, which is 1,500 kilometres inland, the corresponding increase is no more than 50 per cent.

The developing countries of Africa have suffered more than the industrial countries of Europe and North America due to their inability to borrow from the international market and lack of sufficient foreign reserves. The accumulated surpluses of OPEC countries have been placed in European capitals. The need to recycle these surpluses in black Africa cannot be overemphasised.

Oil imports and the Zambian economy

In the first quarter of 1975 Zambia's economy was in dire straits. Foreign exchange reserves were sufficient to cover only three weeks' imports, and the rising cost of imports was beginning to threaten the country's economic stability quite seriously. Whereas the total import bill in 1973 was Kwacha 349 million, it rose in 1974 to Kwacha 502 million, a rise that was largely attributable to increased oil prices. If the price of copper had remained fairly steady at an average price of £900 per metric ton, Zambia's economy would have absorbed the effects of the oil price increases, but this was not to be. During the period between 1970 and 1973 copper production remained fairly constant around 700,000 metric tons, the chief course of fluctuation in export earnings being changes in LME (London Metal Exchange) copper prices. As a result of growing prosperity in the industrial countries, copper had record high prices in October and December 1973. The LME copper price was £1,380 in April 1974, but at the end of the same year the price had fallen to £550. The sharp decline in the price was due to the energy crisis — which caused a sudden drop in world industrial output. Table I shows Zambia's trading patterns:

Table I: Value of Trade in Million Kwacha

Year	Exports	Imports	Trade Surpluses
1970	714.7	340.4	374.3
1971	485.2	399.3	85.9
1972	541.8	403.9	137.9
1973	758.0	350.0	408.0

The figures clearly indicate that Zambia has been doing reasonably well. Copper accounts for 95 per cent of her total exports; other minerals such as zinc, lead and iron ore account for 4 per cent. Agricultural products (such as tobacco) account for 1 per cent. From Table I it can be seen that imports rose rapidly between 1970 and 1971; the bulk of these imports represented consumer goods, a luxury which the country could not afford and therefore in 1972 the government introduced import controls. In 1973 the imports were less than in 1972 because the Rhodesian regime closed the border and therefore Zambia had fewer outlets to the sea. Copper exports were not affected by the border closure because freight charges for copper are higher than on imported goods and therefore port authorities at Lobito, Mozambique and Dar-es-Salaam gave preferential treatment to copper shipments.

Unlike some other African countries who do not have alternative sources of energy, Zambia produces coal at Maamba and hydro-electric energy at Kafue and Kariba Dam. Because of these two other forms of energy Zambia has not suffered to the same extent as those developing countries who depend solely on oil energy.

Before the construction of the refinery at Ndola, the oil products were transported by pipe line. Table II gives the quantities of oil products transported via the pipe line (in tons):

Table II

	1964	1966	1968	1970	1972
Kerosene	4,900	5,800	8,000	12,000	15,300
Aviat. Turb. fuel	5,300	12,000	14,000	16,000	31,900
Premium Mogas	31,000	39,000	48,000	98,000	137,500
Diesel Gasoil	52,000	90,000	180,000	231,000	334,600
Regular Mogas	48,000	58,000	51,000	40,000	45,100
Asphalt	4,800	13,000	19,000	16,000	13,000
Annual Total	146,000	197,800	320,000	413,000	577,900

In June 1973, the refinery was commissioned at the designed capacity of 1.1 million metric tons per annum. The refinery at Ndola supplies oil to the entire Zambian market. Because of great demand for oil created by faster development in the Zambian economy the refinery is expected to reach the design capacity by 1977 instead of 1982 as planned. The forecasts for 1974 and 1975 are shown in Table III.

In 1973 the total cost of oil supply was K61 million and in 1974 it was K123 million. Given good will on the part of the mining industry, it is possible to reduce the consumption of HFO (Heavy Fuel Oil). The government is prepared to introduce savings on regular and premium consumption by restriction of the usage of vehicles. The consumers of HFO are Ndola Copper Refinery, Rhokana Metallurgical Plant, Mufulira Metallurgical Plant, the Glass Factory at Kapiri Mposhi and Ndola Lime. The last two were designed only for HFO, while the copper industry can convert to coal. If the mining companies were to revert to coal and the government decided to introduce saving on regular and premium the country would be saving 90,000 metric tons of HFO and 20 metric tons of mogas;

Table III

	1973	1974	1975
Kerosene	16,600	18,000	19,400
Aviat. Turb. fuel	30,800	32,500	36,900
Premium Mogas	131,800	142,000	152,200
Regular Mogas	44,000	47,400	50,800
Diesel Gasoil	297,900	323,000	349,600
Low Sulphur Gasoil	22,300	23,400	24,500
Bitumen/Asphalt	15,800	15,000	15,000
LPG	9,700	11,900	14,400
Heavy fuel oil	173,700	228,700	247,500
Total:	742,600	941,900	910,300
Refinery fuel and Losses	56,200	64,900	68,800
Grand Total	798,800	906,700	979,100

in money terms this would amount to K8 million. The conversion to coal would increase the demand for coal by about 130,000 metric tons. As stated earlier, the supply of coal is assured because of excess of deposits and excess of capacity at Maamba Colliery. Table IV shows the estimated consumption of oil in Zambia (in thousand metric tons):

Table IV

	1974	%	1975	%	1976	%
Agriculture	12.3	1.3	13.3	1.3	14.2	1.3
Mining	366.7	40.3	397.5	40.5	429.1	40.6
Manufacturing/ Construction	198.1	21.9	205.4	21.0	205.5	19.4
Transport	118.8	13.2	136.2	14.0	162.7	15.4
Commerce/ Services	210.8	23.3	226.7	23.3	244.6	·23.3
	906.7	100.0	979.1	100.0	1056.1	100.0

Since 1973 Zambia has been importing crude oil at a rate of 70,000 metric tons per month. At Dar-es-Salaam before loading into pipelines the crude oil is spiked or blended with naphtha and gas oil, in order to meet the Zambian market requirements for different distillates. The current requirements of the refinery are met by the two supply companies, Shell BP and Agip, each company supplying 50 per cent. The consequences for the Zambian economy of the price increases of Arabian crude were both serious and sustained because copper, which is the mainstay of the economy, consumes about 40 per cent of oil imported into Zambia. Although the supplies to the pipeline have been maintained without difficulty the increase in the cost of imported crude oil had a corresponding effect on the cost of production of copper. Accounts produced by both mining companies, Roan Consolidated Copper Mines and Nchanga Consolidated Copper Mines, show that as a result of the oil price increases their operating costs have gone up. The Minister of Finance, Alexander Chikwanda, recognised this and therefore in his budget speech of 1975 he increased the price of petrol in order to raise K8 million from motorists and other consumers.

For the year 1974 the economic dislocation of the world economy caused by the oil crisis also had a considerable indirect effect on Zambia. Industrial oil consuming countries had to reduce the demand not only for oil but also for other raw materials imported from developing countries. This in turn marked the beginning of a serious economic recession due to a fall in demand. This was inevitable because the oil producers could not spend all the money they earned to generate additional demand. A rapid fall in the demand for copper during the period of continued output expansion caused prices to sag sharply.

Zambia experienced import supply difficulties. The general industrial slowdown by Zambia's traditional suppliers caused great difficulties in obtaining intermediate and capital goods imports necessary to sustain productive sectors in the economy. The acute shortage of fuel and the extra freight surcharge made the transport of supplies more difficult at a time when stocks in Zambia were very low. For the financial year ending 31 December 1975, the country needs K60 million to meet the cost of increased oil prices, according to the budget proposals submitted to Parliament by the Minister of Planning and Finance.

If the world economy was sound, Zambia and other African countries with similar problems would have expected international assistance. Unfortunately aid prospects from industrial countries are bleak.

The effects on Kenya

Before the October War, there were many Israeli nationals carrying on business in different sectors of the Kenyan economy. Kenya was therefore one of the few countries in Africa which were least expected to support the Arab cause. In terms of economics the Kenyans had more to gain from Israel than from the Arabs and yet when the war broke out they voluntarily supported the Arabs.

There are conflicting reports as to which is the country hardest hit by the oil price rises. The International Monetary Fund list places Kenya immediately after Bangladesh and India, whereas the list from the EEC Commission considers that Tanzania and Mali are worst affected. Kenya's economy is more developed than those of Tanzania and Mali and therefore it is not easy to make a direct comparison. You may say that in relative terms the increase in imports of oil for the year ending 31 December 1974 is the same, but in absolute terms Kenya would have imported more oil. Because Kenya's economy is stronger than the other two, she is likely to absorb the shocks of a sudden increase in the price of oil much more than any one of the poorer states. In order to support ambitious economic plans, she has developed a great appetite for oil. Statistics for 1974 show that Kenya's total overseas imports went up from £K203 million in 1973 to £K353 million. The cost of importing oil in 1973 was £K16 million; in 1974 the figure was £K67 million, more than four times as much. Kenya's experience does, however, also show that oil is not the only commodity which has contributed to the present inflation. Looking at detailed foreign trade figures for the first six months of 1973 and 1974, one finds that Kenya's total import bill of all commodities doubled in twelve months. The main increases (apart from oil) were in paper, textiles, iron and steel.

Kenya depends to a very large extent on her tourist industry.

Richard Maina, General Manager of Kenya Tourist and Development Corporation, estimates that between January 1973 and December 1974 there was a 12 per cent decline in the tourist traffic. This means a lot for a country whose tourist industry comes second to coffee as foreign exchange earner, and provides employment to 45,000 Kenyans. Mwai Kibaki, Minister of Finance, says that out of £K1,440 million included in the 1974-8 four year development plan, £K50 million has been estimated for tourism, and out of this sum £K30 million will be spent on the construction of new hotels. Within the period of the plan tourists from Europe will have the opportunity of flying straight to the coast instead of changing planes at Nairobi as is the case now.

There is no doubt that the oil price increases have adversely affected Kenyan tourism. In 1972 (before the increase) tourism netted £K27 million; in 1973 the industry estimates that 500,000 tourists will come to Kenya, 10 per cent more than the estimate for 1974, but it is doubtful whether this target will be reached. The recent air fares increase by all airlines to accommodate the soaring price of oil will make it difficult for average holidaymakers to travel. The increased price of fuel will also throw out of business small transport operators who complement the efforts of Kenya Tourist Development Corporation.

As a temporary measure Kenya has borrowed £K9.2 million from the International Monetary Fund. The rates of interest are concessionary but other terms are unbearable. For every loan obtained from the IMF the Fund demands that apart from cooperating with it in finding appropriate solutions to the borrower's balance of payments problem, the borrower should not impose or intensify restrictions on current international transactions without prior consultation with the Fund. In plain language this means that the borrower, during the period of the loan, will have to accommodate his own exchange control regulations to the requirements of the Fund. In fact, during the period of the loan he is at the mercy of the Fund, whose supervising officers are often inexperienced junior economists.

We have said that the rates of interest are concessionary because they are lower by far than the rates of interest on the

HE Dr Hastings Kamuzu Banda
President of the Republic of Malawi

HH Sheikh Sabah al Salim al Sabah
Amir of the State of Kuwait

open market. For example, Kenya's loan has to be repaid in instalments within a period of seven years and the rate of interest is 6⅞ per cent rising to 7⅛ per cent towards the end of the loan. If it were a Eurodollar loan the rate of interest would not be less than 13 per cent.

In addition to £K9.2 million from the IMF, Kenya has received smaller contributions from the UN´ Emergency Operation Fund and from the Arab Oil Fund. Mwai Kibaki says that the only cure to Kenya's present economic problem lies in the recycling of accumulated oil surpluses into Kenya's economy.

4

African Criticism of the Arabs

An African viewpoint gaining ground is that unless the Arab states change their present attitude to Africa, the continent will continue to look elsewhere for financial assistance. Arab statements of intent have not matched their actions. At the Ministerial Council which met in Addis Ababa in November 1973 (see Chapter 2), the OAU Foreign Ministers resolved to request the Arab heads of state to cut the supply of oil to South Africa, Portugal and Rhodesia. The Arab heads of state met in Algiers from 26 to 29 November 1973 and issued a declaration to the effect that the Arab countries would not only cut the supply of oil to the racist regimes but would also sever diplomatic, consular, economic and cultural relations with those regimes. However, in 1974 it became public knowledge that South Africa, which had been denied the right to buy arms from Britain by the Labour Government, was able to acquire them through the intermediary of Arab countries. The Arab countries concerned did not dare challenge the statement because a denial could have invited further and more damaging disclosures.

On 27 November 1973, Hassan Bulbul, Egyptian Foreign Under-Secretary, issued a statement through the *Egyptian Gazette* pledging financial and technical support to the African countries who had wholeheartedly backed the Arabs during the Israel-Arab conflict. He said:

There should be cooperation between the Arab world and the African countries. Africa can offer raw materials while the Arabs can offer the expertise and capital; for example, Africa has about 200 million feddans of potential arable lands ready for reclamation, whereas the Arabs have the agricultural expertise . . . As for the industrial field, the Arab countries buy enormous quantities of such raw materials as timber, iron and steel, aluminium, coffee and tea from some European and Asian countries, while Africa is a close and cheap market for the Arabs.

He added that trade between them would be for mutual advantage.

Statements like that encouraged many African leaders to visit Arab countries. Despite the fact that some delegations included their heads of state, they returned home poorer than they had been before they undertook such tours. A delegation consisting of six people travelling economy class by air from Botswana to Beirut may not mean much to an Arab sheikh but the same expenditure would represent a sizeable percentage to the budget of a country like Botswana.

The trade, financial and technical cooperation that Hassan Bulbul was referring to appears to have been directed to Europe and not Africa. This conclusion stems from the fact that since that statement was made, Arabs and Iranians have invested billions of dollars in Europe and the United States. These investments include 100 million dollars in Krupp Steel, a German company; 400 million dollars in Daimler-Benz, another German company; 1.2 million in Mereworth Castle, a residence for the United Arab Emirates in England; 300 million dollars in Pan American World Airways and about 1,800 million dollars in small loans to various businesses in Europe and the US. Africa is still waiting for the Arab mind to change its course. For the moment it is apparently fixed on two continents, Europe and North America. To most of the Arab states Africa remains the dark continent.

During their meeting in November 1973, the Arab heads of state said that in appreciation of the support they had received from member-states of the OAU, they were going to give financial assistance to African states. They planned to do this by setting up an Arab-African financial organisation 'which will share in the plans for economic and social development and the supply of technical aid to the countries of Africa. The Arab Economics Ministers will lay down the rules of the organisation and the amount of its capital.'

Later in 1973 the secretary-general of the Arab League met representatives of the OAU from Botswana, Cameroon, Ghana, Mali, Sudan, Tanzania and Zaire to discuss the setting up of this 'Arab Bank for Industrial and Agricultural Development in Africa' with a suggested capital of 125 million dollars and an 'Arab technical assistance fund'. After criticism from Tanzania's Foreign Minister, John Malecela, and others the Bank's initial capital was raised to 231 million dollars. This was agreed at the Afro-Arab Cooperation Conference in Cairo in January 1974. Also agreed was the establishment of a 200 million dollar Arab Loan Fund, which after much delay has now been made available to the African Development Bank to allocate to individual countries according to their needs. The loans carry an interest of 1 per cent and are repayable over five years, with a three-year grace period. On top of this is a technical assistance fund of 15 million dollars. (The only known commitment in early 1975 was 2 million dollars from the United Arab Emirates.) These commitments amount to a total of 446 million dollars, which developing Africa can borrow over eight years. But with Africa's oil bill rising at well over that amount each year over the next ten years, 446 million dollars is a drop in the ocean. A fairly representative African view was expressed by the *Standard* (Nairobi) on 7 August 1974, when it said: 'So it looks as if, in spite of Arab generosity, we are still going to have to find nine-tenths of the increased oil bill.' (However, to be fair, it was reported by *African Development* (London) in June 1975 that the Arab League was replenishing its fund each year at an annual rate of 200 million dollars.)

The heads of states of OPEC countries held a meeting in Algiers in March 1975; they reviewed the present world economic and financial crisis. They discussed in great depth its causes and formulated measures which would not only safeguard the interest of their own people but also the interest of all the peoples of the world. As in the past, they made certain declarations designed to help the least developed countries of the Third World. Africans are keen to read and hear about these statements, which are eloquently presented, but they are neither moved nor impressed by such statements; they want action rather than words.

Let us look at some of the Algiers decisions. First and foremost, they wanted to tell the world that their action to increase the price of oil was fair and just. It was designed to protect the legitimate rights of their peoples. They contended that they had acted in the direction hoped for by all developing countries, producers of raw materials, in defence of the legitimate rights of their people. The African peoples respect the rights of OPEC members to do whatever they want with their raw materials; these rights include increasing the price of oil or reducing the quantity of production so long as their actions do not cripple the economies of other developing countries whom they are professing to help. It is common knowledge that the present Arab decisions are at variance with the economic aspirations of the African peoples.

The heads of state recognised that the present world economic crisis stems from the profound inequalities in the economic and social progress among peoples. According to them, the inequalities which characterise the underdevelopment of the developing countries are in the main due to the absence of adequate international cooperation for development. It is certainly regrettable to note that the rich Arab countries are now the main contributors to the basic disequilibrium in economic relations. Their present policy of investing in Europe and America means that they are taking coals to Newcastle, or in other words, they are rechannelling capital to areas where it is least needed.

The Africans agree with the Arabs that the oil producing countries are not solely responsible for the disequilibrium now affecting the present international community. The main cause lies in the fact that the industrial countries have been prone to excessive consumption of luxurious goods and to a wasteful use of scarce resources. When it comes to conspicuous consumption it is doubtful whether the newly rich Arabs who claim to be conservative in their tastes are any different from their affluent European and American counterparts. It is widely known that salesmen from Europe and America are flocking to the Middle East to trade and deal on a scale undreamed of by the sheikhs. Any salesman who comes back from the Middle East with less than 10 million dollars of orders would not consider his selling trip as having been successful. As one salesman put it: 'The Arabs are getting so rich that they will soon have to find a common currency with a basic unit of one million dollars, so that they can count quickly.'

The Arabs recognise that there is a close relationship

between their economies and those of the rest of the world, and therefore they are aware and mindful of the difficulties being experienced by peoples of the world community. But are they doing anything to alleviate the squalor and misery which continue to exist in the least developed countries of the world? Africa, together with other developing countries of Asia, Latin America, the Caribbean and the Pacific, are the main producers of raw materials for the industries of Europe and North America where the Arabs are investing most of their funds.

In view of the unity of purpose now being shown through various economic councils and conventions such as UNCTAD and the present Lome Convention, it will not be long before the countries of the Third World are in a position to exercise economic power similar to the present Arab economic power. It is therefore an absolute necessity for the Arabs to extend their dialogue and cooperation on economic matters to the developing countries of Africa. At the moment, the dialogue is restricted to the developed countries of Europe and America. The Arab countries have generously assisted the industrial countries financially in order to meet their balance of payments deficits. While Europe and America have been assisted by loans which carry concessionary rates of interest of about 5 per cent, African countries have to borrow the same funds on the Eurodollar markets at rates of interest which fluctuate between 15 per cent and 20 per cent.

When the Arabs are asked about their plans to help the Africans, their reply is standard: 'We are committed to help our African brothers. We have decided to coordinate their programmes for financial cooperation in order to assist them to overcome their balance of payments difficulties. We have also decided to coordinate such financial measures with long-term loans that will contribute to the development of those economies.'

Between January 1974 and March 1975 I visited several countries in Africa, travelling extensively in West, East and Central Africa. I was informed by government ministers and senior officials that they have been waiting for financial assistance from their Arab friends for too long. Most of them had even lost hope of ever getting it.

A common Arab viewpoint is that their territories are

developing countries and therefore they cannot afford to be charitable with their funds. Obviously, Africa does not expect gifts of dollars like manna from heaven, but I think it is fair to say that Arab governments think that financial assistance is synonymous with financial aid. It is important to point out that for operational purposes, financial assistance refers to money loaned on concessionary rates of interest. It is not a gift; it has to be repaid. This type of loan is supposed to supplement the efforts of the borrower. Financial aid, on the other hand, is generally a gift or loan given, interest free, for an indefinite period. African governments are quite prepared to repay loans with interest within a stipulated period and would be grateful for terms such as the Arab nations have been offering European countries.

I have met many responsible Arabs who believe that it is the exclusive duty of Africa's former colonial masters to offer aid to their former colonies and that they are bound to compensate those countries which they had exploited. Industrial countries without a colonial legacy may also offer financial aid and assistance to the developing countries of the world. President Nasser subscribed to this train of thought. He once said:

> In their conscious revolutionary outlook, our people consider it the duty of the advanced states to offer aid to those still struggling for development; and in their conception of history, our people believe that states with a colonialist past should, more than others, offer to the nations aspiring to development part of the national wealth they sapped when that wealth was a booty for all looters. Offering aid is the duty of the advanced states. It is almost a form of tax payable by the states with a colonialist past to compensate those they exploited for so long.

President Nasser himself recognised that in the modern world foreign capital is a prerequisite for economic development, because it is often accompanied by technological know-how. He said: 'Foreign capital as an investment is accepted in indispensable operations, especially those requiring new experience difficult to find in the national domain.'

Before the Arab governments recognised that the wealth underneath them was capable of turning them overnight into multimillionaires, they believed, and rightly so, that foreign investment in Arab territories was a necessary component in their economic development. Hence they allowed foreign firms to carry out exploration and prospecting for oil. Nasser and other Arab leaders did everything possible to attract foreign aid as long as it had no strings attached; in other words it was not used as an instrument for neo-colonialism. In support of foreign aid he said:

> Foreign capital and its role in local investment is a question we should deal with at this stage. Foreign capital is regarded with dark doubts in underdeveloped countries, particularly those which were colonised. However, the sovereignty of the people over their land, and their regaining of control, allow them to define the conditions under which foreign capital may be invested in their country. The matter calls for the setting up of a system drawn from the essence of the national experience. It also takes into account the nature of world capital which is always striving after unexploited raw materials in areas not yet ready for any economic or social revival, where it can obtain the highest rate of interest.
>
> In the first place, in the process of national evolution, all foreign aid with no strings attached is accepted to help attain the national objectives. This aid is accepted with sincere gratitude to those who offer it, regardless of the colour of their flags. In the second place, in the process of national evolution, all unconditional loans are accepted provided they can be refunded without difficulty or strain. Experience shows that loans are a straightforward operation; their problem completely ends with their amortisation and the reimbursement of the interest due.

Throughout the period of writing this book, I have been preoccupied with the question of why the Arabs are keen to rescue the European economy and only to pay lip-service to the African economy, why they are willing to establish a long-term partnership with Europe and not with Africa, a partnership which will stimulate economic growth for Europe and not for Africa. As one African diplomat put it: 'The biggest transfer of wealth in history is now taking place from the Middle East to Europe. The proletarian nations of Africa are mere spectators in the entire drama.' Presumably, the answer to my question lies in the statement made by Dr Sadun Hamad, the Oil Minister of Iraq, when he said:

My country is not opposed to the policy of oil cutbacks, but as producers of oil we must think of the future and must set the ceiling to which we can allow prices to rise. The industrialised nations which need oil possess gigantic scientific potential, and have alternative sources of energy for the future. We cannot expect to place the economies of the industrialised nations in danger without expecting a backlash.

At the height of the oil war in 1973, a leading Egyptian journalist, Hassanein Heikal, asked the Arab countries to lift the oil embargo on Europe because the action was not achieving the desired effect. He said: 'Europe is incapable of putting pressure on the United States as the Arabs wanted and, cost what it may, the Common Market countries will maintain solidarity. We cannot ask of Europe what it cannot give; if we do, we are imposing an undeserved punishment.' The construction to be placed on the statements of Dr Hamad and Mr Heikal is that the Arabs cannot long inflict punishment on Europe because it has the stamina to hit back and it has sufficient scientific potential to come up with alternative methods of generating other sources of energy. Even the *Development Forum*, a publication of the United Nations, had this to say in its issue of December 1973:

The developing countries are going to suffer most and longest from the energy crisis since apart from the oil producing states like Nigeria and Indonesia, some 75 per cent of them do not produce their own energy supplies. The least developed countries will carry the heaviest burdens because they have nothing to fall back

on, like rich coal deposits, no technology to speed the
development of new resources such as nuclear or solar
energy, and no financial means to meet the rising cost of
oil . . . Oil, which flows so easily from wells to pipeline into
tanker, refinery and pump, and eventually into furnace or
generator, is a convenience for the industrial countries;
for the developing world it is a lifeline essential to its
survival.

The *Development Forum* is also saying in different words that
the developing world at the moment has no scientific potential
to develop alternative methods of generating new forms of
energy because of its financial embarrassment.

It may be argued that the Arabs are members of the Third
World and therefore by definition they need money to develop
their economies. It is true that if one is talking about
technological development, the Arab world belongs to the Third
World, but in terms of money they rank with the richest
countries of Europe and America. According to conservative
estimates the Arab oil producers, after meeting their
international contractual obligations and after meeting all the
expenses related to their annual recurrent expenditure and the
expenditure of their various development projects, are likely to
accumulate 200 to 250 billion dollars by the end of this decade.

5

Various Proposals for Recycling the Accumulated Surplus of Arab Oil Money

During the year 1974 all economic and political misfortunes were attributed to abnormal increases in the price of oil. World leaders' knowledge was judged on how they were able to articulate on economic issues arising from Arab oil inflation. Conferences were called to discuss ways and means of recycling vast surpluses accumulated by the Middle East oil producers. The OPEC countries met in Vienna in September 1974 and resolved that instead of increasing the price of oil they were going to impose increased taxes on companies operating within the territories of OPEC countries (the increase in tax was 5 per cent). An international Conference on Energy was arranged in Detroit. The twelve industrial countries of the world, which included Japan, the US, Norway and the member-states of the EEC (excluding France) met in September and agreed to share oil stocks in the event of future shortages. In November, countries of Africa, the Caribbean and the Pacific (ACP) meeting in Brussels agreed to collaborate with oil producing countries in order to alleviate the shortage of oil in their respective countries.

It is common knowledge that any conference which lacks the participation of the Arab oil producing countries cannot adequately handle the problem of production and price of oil. Since the Arabs own and control huge oil reserves they inevitably hold the key to economic development in a developing continent like Africa. Without oil energy, most of Africa's newly formulated development plans will have to be shelved in their national archives.

The Secretariat of the OAU has taken a keen interest in various proposals made by Western countries to recycle vast accumulated reserves by the Middle East oil producers. In

51

September 1974, the West German Finance Minister, Hans
Apel, submitted to the annual meeting of the International
Monetary Fund his country's proposal that under the
supervision of the IMF, the oil producing countries and the
industrial nations should establish an International Investment
Bank to help recycle the surplus oil revenue. The term
'recycling' is used here to mean ploughing back money into the
consumers' economies. The Minister emphasised his government's cherished view that there should be no animosity or
confrontation between the two parties, the consumers and the
producers.

The American proposal was more elaborate than the German
one. The basic tenet of the American plan was to break up an oil
cartel that threatens to destroy the Western economy. Her
proposal was that the Western countries should conserve oil by
reducing consumption. They should embark on new energy
programmes aimed at discovering alternative sources of power.
They should establish a 25 billion dollar fund to recycle Arab oil
money into deficit countries. The fund would be controlled by
consumers and not by producers. This means that when the
council charged with the responsibility of managing the fund
meets to discuss contributions to the fund, producer countries
would be invited to attend, but when the council meets to
discuss the disbursement of funds, producer countries would be
excluded. The US intended to implement her recommendation
by relying on the price mechanism. She would increase Federal
Petrol Tax and impose higher tariffs on imported oil; both
taxes would mean higher prices to users and consumers. The
main US intention is to influence the production, pricing and
selling policies of OPEC countries.

The British would like to work within the framework of the
IMF. They have proposed an IMF oil surplus fund of between
6,000 million dollars and 12,000 million dollars. This would be
supplementary to other international funds set up for the same
purpose. The proposal includes a recommendation to recycle
trade surpluses within the OECD group. They have also
recommended an increase in IMF quotas for industrial and oil
producing countries. The quotas for less developed countries
would remain the same. The borrowing rights are based on the
countries' quotas. Under the present arrangement IMF rules

provide that a member-country should produce 25 per cent of its subscription in gold. The British are recommending that since gold cannot be considered as the prime measure of value it should be phased out of the IMF system. As far as the African countries are concerned the British proposal has one disadvantage. Since the borrowing rights are based on the IMF quota system and since the less developed countries will not increase their quotas, the less developed countries would not benefit from this method of recycling. They would have to borrow comparatively less money from the IMF.

France, on the other hand, is cautious. She does not want to associate herself with a decision which may infuriate the Arab oil countries. She has held a view that any consumer alliance formed by the industrial countries alone would lead to punitive action by the oil producing countries. France wants a conference to include producers, consumers and the countries of the Third World. The first attempt at such a conference in April 1975 was a failure, with delegates unable to agree on what to discuss. The Americans were held largely responsible for the failure.

The International Energy Agency and its opponents

On 27 May 1975, what the British newspaper the *Guardian* described as 'episode 94 of the great oil saga began in Paris, with Dr Kissinger promoting the US-backed International Energy Agency (IEA) to secure unity of purpose and action among the developed oil consuming nations. The previous month the oil producers and developing nations had refused to attend a conference with official IEA participation. Algerian spokesmen described the IEA as ''an agency of confrontation'' — a view backed by the rest of the Third World.' Since US spokesmen had appeared on television to declare that their government's policy was to break up OPEC, and there had been heavy hints of possible US military intervention to take over key Middle East oilfields, it was hardly surprising that any American-backed scheme was treated with extreme suspicion by OPEC countries.

But the May 1975 IEA and OECD meetings (which were held on consecutive days) unveiled a less belligerent Dr Kissinger than had been expected. He proposed to reopen talks between producers and consumers, and more remarkable was his support for new aid to the Third World amounting to 3,000 million dollars. He told OECD delegates that the rich nations must lend a hand to the Third World or face 'dangerous political pressures'. Economic issues were turning into central political issues. On the other hand, he refused to veer from the traditional US view that the 1973 'oil war' was misused economic power that threatened stability in the West, adding: 'The US will resist block pressure tactics, but will try to accommodate the interests of the developing countries.' The 3,000 million dollar aid figure would be made up of a 2,000 million dollar trust fund within the IMF to help the poorest nations buy energy, food, fertilisers and industrial goods, and a 1,000 million dollar International Fund for Agricultural Development, as proposed by the oil producers.

The most important US concession to Third World feelings was the tacit agreement to consider all Third World commodity prices and not merely oil. There is thus a chance of a new form of cooperation being worked out, perhaps more in line with France's thinking on the subject than appeared possible a month earlier.

The view of the OAU

The Secretariat of the OAU supports France's stand. The organisation believes that the problem of recycling oil money should benefit all members of the international community. Hence the problem cannot be resolved by bilateral arrangements. The real solution can only be found in massive international action. In other words, countries of the Third World must be an integral part of the decision making. This stand by the OAU should not be construed to mean that the organisation is opposed to any bilateral financial or economic assistance to any country of the Third World. On the contrary, the Organisation would like to encourage individual Arab countries to give preferential treatment to countries like Tanzania and Mali which have been among the most badly hit by oil price increases.

The basic African criticism of the American plan is that its proposed consumer block is seen by OPEC as confrontation and not as a means of solving the problem. If the oil producing countries are going to be asked to contribute to a 25 billion dollar fund to recycle their receipts into deficit countries it is right and fair that they be allowed to participate in the management of the fund. For 1974 the proposed 25 billion dollar fund fell short of the estimated deficit of 31 billion dollars by industrial countries. The estimate for OPEC countries was a surplus of 65 billion dollars. It follows that industrial countries without the support of OPEC countries would not balance their books. According to the US, the energy sharing agreement (to be a standby arrangement in the case of new embargoes) would be restricted to industrial countries. This subtle discrimination would not sell to the countries of the Third World; one is inclined to think that the countries of OPEC would not entertain such a proposal.

The German proposal in its present form cannot be sold to African countries. It provided that membership of the International Investment Bank would be restricted to oil producing nations and industrial countries. Countries of the Third World have been equally adversely affected by inflation. If they were able to join IMF there is no reason why they cannot be members of a fund that is lower in status. After all, their colleagues in OPEC will probably contribute a greater portion of the fund. One African diplomat of long standing in Bonn said that the West German proposal was not intended to serve countries of the Third World. She is more concerned with some member-states in the EEC, such as the UK and Italy, which are burdened with huge balance of payments deficits. In 1974 the Bundesbank loaned Italy 2,000 million dollars. The German government does not want to deplete her reserves by giving financial assistance to EEC member-states. She wants this task to be undertaken by both industrial countries and the oil producing countries.

The EEC contribution to the UN Emergency Fund

Claude Cheysson, the EEC Commissioner for Development and Cooperation has announced that the EEC is to contribute 500 million dollars to an Emergency Fund set up by the Secretary General of the UN. Apparently this decision was conditional upon other members of the UN contributing the remaining 2,500 million. The money will be distributed to countries of the

Third World which are unable to balance their budgets as a result of quadrupled oil prices. The following African countries will benefit from this fund: Dahomey, Ivory Coast, Ghana, Guinea, Upper Volta, Kenya, Lesotho, Madagascar, Mali, Mauritania, Niger, Central African Republic, Tanzania, Cameroon, Senegal, Sierra Leone, Somalia, Sudan and Chad. Initially the EEC will release 150 million dollars.

Mr Cheysson added that in June 1974 the EEC Council of Ministers had already sent a letter to the UN Secretary General informing him that the EEC was going to make its contribution in an amount not exceeding 500 million dollars. It was expected that the total fund could be 3,000 million dollars, made up as follows: EEC 500 million dollars; United States 500 million dollars; other industrial countries 500 million dollars; and 1,500 million dollars by the oil producing countries. The Commission was surprised to learn that the US was delaying in making a decision about her contribution to the fund. But in May 1975 the US finally agreed to make up its share.

The negotiations between ACP and EEC for associate membership of the Community have enabled EEC member-states to appreciate the economic problems of ACP countries. For example, the French Development Minister, Pierre Abelin, who visited Africa during 1974, emphasised that African countries should be placed on the priority list of the countries to benefit from the EEC contribution. He observed that according to the Commission's figures, Mali and Tanzania were the most seriously affected. According to him, unless the industrial countries come to their rescue, Tanzania would have to reduce her imports by 17 per cent in 1974 and 1975 and Mali would have to reduce her imports by 30 per cent in 1974 and 25 per cent in 1975. Their development budgets would have to be reduced accordingly.

International economic cooperation

In pursuance of his cherished ambition, Valery Giscard d'Estaing, President of the Republic of France, on 16 December 1975, convened a Conference on International Economic Cooperation.

The Conference was unique in that, for the first time, the entire complex of economic problems would be examined on a

HE Al Hajji Field Marshal Idi Amin Dada
President of the Republic of Uganda

HE President Mohamed Anwar Sadat of Egypt

global scale. Numerous meetings which had preceded it had confined themselves to specialised fields.

Representatives from OAU were anxiously waiting for the results of this Conference because the Conference was charged with the responsibilities of resolving problems of energy, raw materials, aid for development and finance. All these matters could be examined and tabled from the standpoint of producers and consumers, that of the industrial and developing countries, as well as of donor and recipient countries.

The aim of the Conference was to promote reason and justice in the functioning of the world economy. The Conference noted that unpredictability prevailed in today's world economy; consequently, the investor hesitates to commit himself; the importer restricts himself to immediate orders and the exporter inflates his prices as a precaution against an uncertain future. Greater stability and good monetary relations were essential as the basis for stable measurement of value and for calculating the profitability of investment.

The second aim was to achieve a more orderly evolution of the prices of products constituting a significant proportion of international trade whether raw materials or industrial products.

There was also the related need to safeguard the value of export earnings of the developing producers to enable the smooth and predictable implementation of development programmes. Special attention was necessary to accommodate the particular circumstances and requirements of the most seriously affected or poorest developing countries.

The major task of the Conference as a whole was to lay down a new approach which would characterise the future relations among developed and developing countries so as to achieve equitable progress and prosperity.

The importance of maximum international economic cooperation is self-evident. A radical change in this regard is needed if the world economy is to satisfy the eminent demands projected for the future. If as predicted by some experts, the world population will nearly double between 1970 and 2000, the world community will need double the present food production, double the social amenities, double the energy and double the jobs. The fullest measure of international economic cooperation is therefore an essential precondition.

The Conference set up four committees to deal with energy, raw materials, development and finance.

Energy

The Conference agreed that to enable the achievement of smooth functioning of world economy and economic development, consistent with the interests of rich and poor countries, there is need to share information on energy in order to enable the identification of essential energy problems. This would in turn enable the formulation of sound arrangements for international cooperation. It would, above all, make better use of current and foreseeable resources.

The delegation of the United Kingdom stated that by 1980, the UK will be the second largest oil producer — after the United States — in the western world. They expect to produce 45 per cent of total energy resources of the European Community. They expect to be self-sufficient in energy supply by 1980.

The issue of energy received prominent comment particularly from OPEC member delegations. Mention was made that the era of cheap energy was long gone. The price of energy had been kept at very low levels for a long time. The producers of oil were entitled to protect their natural resources, particularly those which are non-renewable, to fix a fair price for their exports, and to protect their income from the erosion of their purchasing power.

The oil producers asserted that the developed countries had reacted to the energy crisis with confrontation, whereas they were willing and desired to resolve problems on the basis of cooperation. To this extent, the developed countries had made efforts to conserve energy with the malicious intention of undermining the interests of the OPEC countries.

The oil producers stated that they had provided far more financial assistance to the developing countries, including the most seriously affected, than the developed countries, on the basis of their aggregate GNP in 1974 (2 per cent). In this connection, non-oil producing countries made reference to the vulnerability of the developing countries to increased oil prices. The majority of them were burdened with serious balance of payments deficits. It was stated that the current account deficit of the developing countries now roughly corresponds to the current account surplus of the oil exporting countries.

The Conference was urged not to disregard this reality when solutions were proposed and examined with a view to overcoming the present crisis.

The remarks made regarding the impact of high oil prices particularly on the non-oil producing countries were made within the broad interpretation of crisis, including the adverse impact of inflation, food and fertiliser shortages and high prices. Consequently, the effect of observations on the oil situation was somewhat minimised. It was significant, however, that developing member delegations spoke with candour on this issue.

Raw Materials

The views expressed on this issue were familiar, and reflected established facts. This subject was also widely debated.

Emphasis was placed on the importance of raw material export trade to developing countries. In this regard, concern was expressed on the adverse impact of price fluctuations on the economies of developing countries. Accordingly, it was advocated that a formula which satisfied the needs of both producers and consumers be established.

It was observed that inflation and economic recession in the OECD countries, which taken as a whole import 75 per cent of the products exported by the developing countries, is a factor which severely restricted international trade. In addition, mention was made of the worsening terms of trade between manufactured goods and raw materials or commodities in general.

In a statement, the situation facing the raw materials export trade was highlighted. Urgent action was urged to enable the speedy setting up of international commodity stocking arrangements as well as providing for their financing. The world food problem was also given priority mention.

Development

There were no specific comments on this subject apart from general passing references to it in observations on other subjects.

Finance

Emphasis was placed on the need to dispense real resource transfers on a continuous, steadily increasing and assured basis so as to enable the smooth execution of development programmes in the developing countries.

The Conference decided to initiate an intensified international dialogue. To this end, it established four Commissions (on energy, raw materials, development and financial affairs) which will meet periodically through the coming year. It was agreed that each of the four Commissions should consist of fifteen members, ten of them representing developing countries, five of them representing industrialised countries.

The Conference agreed that the following participants should serve on the Commissions:

Energy: Algeria, Brazil, Canada, Egypt, EEC, India, Iran, Iraq, Jamaica, Japan, Saudi Arabia, Switzerland, United States, Venezuela and Zaire.

Raw Materials: Argentina, Australia, Cameroon, EEC, Indonesia, Japan, Mexico, Nigeria, Peru, Spain, United States, Yugoslavia and Zaire.

Finance: Brazil, EEC, Egypt, India, Indonesia, Iran, Iraq, Japan, Mexico, Pakistan, Saudi Arabia, Sweden, Switzerland, United States and Zambia.

The co-Chairmen of the Commissions will be:
Energy: Saudi Arabia and United States
Raw Materials: Japan and Peru
Development: Algeria and EEC
Finance: EEC and Iran

6
What the Arabs can do for Africa

A senior Arab diplomat in Bonn has said that the Arab oil producing countries are aware of the chronic poverty of some African countries. They are also aware that for the years 1974 and 1975 most African countries will have deficit balance of payments caused by increased import costs and 'to a certain extent' by the increase in the price of oil. The diplomat refused to accept the allegation that inflation in Africa is due to quadrupled oil prices. He argued that European countries which had colonised Africa left an economic structure which is dependent on finished products from the western countries. The economies of newly independent states of Africa are designed to produce raw materials for export to Europe. These are sold at lamentably low prices. These raw materials are turned into finished products which are exported to Africa at exorbitant prices. In his view, Africa is a victim of imported inflation from Europe and the US.

Other things being equal, Arab countries would like to directly subsidise less developed economies of Africa by selling oil to them at a reduced price. But they cannot do this because such a system would be exploited by multinational companies operating in Africa. If you are selling in an open market you cannot introduce discriminatory prices and hope to succeed in achieving the objective of getting the cheap product to the man who deserves it. The OPEC countries have weighed this proposal and found it wanting.

To minimise the hardship among African countries the Arab oil countries have agreed in principle to offer development aid to African countries. They have also agreed to invest in local industries of some selected African countries.

After discussions with several leaders of OPEC countries, one gets the impression that these privileged members of the Third World are not unprepared to assist their less fortunate brothers. For example, in June 1974, representatives of the

OPEC countries met in Quito, Ecuador. At this meeting they resolved that the increase in prices of oil was doing more harm than good to the countries of the Third World. Countries of Africa, in particular, had suffered more than industrial countries of Europe which owned and controlled multinational oil companies. It was therefore decided not to increase prices of oil; instead they agreed to impose taxes on profits and royalties of foreign companies operating in OPEC areas. At a subsequent meeting in Vienna, taxes were again increased.

Before the Quito meeting, taxes were 12.5 per cent on royalties and 55 per cent on profits. After the meeting taxes were 14.5 per cent on royalties and no change on tax on profits. The Vienna meeting increased the royalty tax to 16.6 per cent and profit tax to 66.66 per cent. But some of the economic laws are immutable. The incidence of such taxes did not fall on the operating companies because the companies in turn increased the price of oil, hence the impact of profit and royalty taxes was felt by the ultimate consumers, who were to pay higher prices for oil.

When I mentioned that the Arab countries had committed certain aid to Africa during a conversation with a senior executive of Commerz Bank, one of the largest German banks, he replied that according to information available to his bank the amounts I was referring to were negligible. He estimated that the Arab countries had so far invested 15 billion dollars all over the world, 7 billion dollars in the US, 3 billion dollars to the UK (mainly office property) and 5 billion dollars in the European banking system. He said that Arabs had invested more in industrial countries than in the countries of the Third World. In his view Africa did not have many profitable industries in which Arab money could be invested. In Europe, the US and Britain they have invested in stocks and shares, real estate and commercial banking. Africa (minus South Africa) does not have developed markets and therefore investments will have to be channelled in government control-led enterprises which are not profitable.

A businessman resident in the UK who has invested a lot of money in Africa said to me that at present the Arab oil investments in Africa have been restricted to the African Development Bank, the Islamic Bank and the Arab Bank for

Africa. He said that there are many ways by which Arab oil countries can assist their African brothers. For example, they can generously contribute to an international fund like the one recently established by the United Nations, or they can take equity participation in state owned development banks or enterprises, or they can on their own set up industries in various African countries. If they want a good return on their investment they can together with the host government set up companies to exploit Africa's abundant minerals.

The businessman said that his Arab business associates had informed him that the OPEC countries had agreed to give loans to the following international organisations: the International Monetary Fund 3,400 million dollars; World Bank 1,000 million dollars; International American Development Bank 500 million dollars. They had also earmarked 3,000 million dollars for the less fortunate Middle East countries. The total of these amounts might appear large, but is, however, a drop in the ocean when one considers for 1974 alone the Arab oil net receipts are estimated to be in the region of 80,000 million dollars (after taking into account their own purchases of industrial plant, arms, prestigious limousines and various social amenities).

OECD suggestions for development cooperation

The 1974 review of efforts and policies of the members of the OECD Development Assistance Committee spells out the situation in the developing countries by suggesting that they adapt to the increases in the oil prices by the development of indigenous energy resources, by reviewing domestic investment priorities and technologies and by increasing their export potential to earn the additional foreign exchange required to pay for the increased oil bill. It adds: 'These structural adaptations require time.' This is small comfort for the majority of African states who are too preoccupied with present disruption to plan ahead meaningfully, but the OECD report adds: 'The decisions which now need to be made about developing countries' future energy policies are of far-reaching importance for the future development of these countries, since the investments involved are very large in relation to the countries' total resource availabilities.' The OECD thinks that private foreign investment may have an important role to play not only in providing the technology, but also in financing the major investments required. It goes on to propose some form of investment by the oil producers in the developing oil consuming nations. In the context of facilitating this flow of private capital it suggests: 'The industrialised countries and the international capital markets should act as intermediaries for the recycling of part of the financial surplus of oil producing countries to the other developing countries.' In suggesting ways of encouraging the direct flow of investment from oil producing countries to other developing countries the OECD's report has this to say:

> National and international institutions with experience in these fields might assist, if requested, in the establishment of national investment and lending institutions, investment guarantee schemes and other incentives by oil producing countries. Industrialised countries and international institutions should also take all possible opportunities for joint investment by investors of industrial and oil producing countries with the possible participation of investors of developing countries.

7
Possible Areas of Investment in Africa

In February 1975, Robert Gardiner, the former executive secretary of the Economic Commission for Africa (ECA) addressed
delegates in Nairobi who had come from countries of East and
Central Africa. He said that one does not need to pursue an
intelligent man about investing his money. The Arabs, like any-
one else, are looking for an investment opportunity. In his view,
Arabs are not going to throw their money away. 'Africans must
have their projects ready; must bargain for funds, for loans, to
implement their projects, on the understanding that the projects
will become viable and they will be able to pay both the capital
and interest. So, the money, if it goes to Europe or anywhere else
is because you have institutions in Europe, you have the people
who are prepared to pay for the money.' Mr Gardiner believes
that if the African countries had industry to sustain Arab oil
money investments, the money would go to them. And if they
are aware that they do not have facilities then they must create
the facilities. Mr Gardiner's view is an optimistic one in view of
the continuing dependence of most developing African countries
on overseas advice, whether from the UN or from private
consultants. However, those countries with adequate indigenous
planning machinery should take heed of Mr Gardiner's words.

From the angle of interesting Arab investors in Africa's plen-
tiful raw materials, it is hard to see why African countries should
have any difficulties at all. In 1975 Saudi Arabia launched a massive 142,000 million dollar five-year plan which included proposals for setting up entirely new industrial complexes, one at
Jabail in the East and another at Yanbu on the Red Sea. The
projects listed for these complexes include a steelworks, an iron
smelter and a cement plant. Since Africa's reserves of iron ore
are said (by the US Treasury) to total twice those of the US and
two-thirds those of the USSR, it would seem natural for a
country like Saudi Arabia to look across the Red Sea to Africa

for a permanent source of supply for that essential raw material. Iron ore is Africa's most widely distributed mineral, and is found in commercial quantities in Algeria, Angola, Egypt, Ghana, Guinea, Ivory Coast, Liberia, Mauritania, Morocco, Namibia, Nigeria, Rhodesia, Sierra Leone, Swaziland and Zambia. But the list of mineral producing countries does not end there. Although up to the present South Africa has seemed to control a wide variety of the market in African minerals, with its gold, chromite, iron ore, platinum, diamonds, nickel, manganese, asbestos, coal and zinc, it is no longer dominant. Even gold is not a purely South African mineral, being found also in the Congo Republic, Ethiopia, Gabon, Ghana, Kenya, Namibia, Rhodesia, Sudan, Tanzania and Zaire. Diamonds are also widespread through Botswana, the Central African Republic, Ghana, Ivory Coast, Liberia, Namibia, Sierra Leone, Tanzania and Zaire.

Of the minerals that are becoming increasingly vital to industrial output, like bauxite (for aluminium) and copper, Africa has some of the world's most extensive reserves. Copper is currently being mined in Algeria, Angola, Mauritania, Morocco, Uganda and most significantly in Zaire and Zambia, while bauxite workings are being opened up at a rapid pace in both Ghana and Guinea. Indeed President Sekou Toure claims that Guinea has two-thirds of the world's known bauxite reserves. The foreign companies already exploiting Guinea's bauxite range from American to Swiss, Yugoslav and Russian. In 1974 Guinea hosted the first meeting of the International Bauxite Association, a body of producers modelled on the oil producers' OPEC.

Other minerals of which Africa is a major source are uranium, phosphates, nickel, cobalt, tungsten, chromite, tin, lead, manganese and zinc.

Apart from its mineral resources, Africa is a major producer and exporter of agricultural products. Perhaps the main cash crop is coffee (the US takes 33 per cent of its coffee from Africa) followed by cocoa (West Africa is the world's main cocoa growing area). Groundnuts thrive in the sub-Sahelian belt of West Africa, from Senegal to the Sudan, as well as in Mozambique. Tobacco and sugar are largely southern and central African crops although recent projects have introduced both on a commercial scale further north. Oil palm and rubber are found in the forest regions from the coast of Senegal as far south as Zambia. Cotton is an extremely widespread crop, most successfully produced by Egypt, Sudan and Uganda.

As far as producing its own food is concerned, Africa still has a long way to go, but if properly planned Africa's agricultural production could easily feed the entire world. Massive research and investment is still needed. Meanwhile the fishing industry is already becoming a major African activity.

An area in which the new Arab wealth could be of immediate and direct benefit both to Africa and the Arabs is in industry. Many of the wealthiest Arab oil producing countries have a restricted land area and small populations. To locate industries in heavy concentrations along the Persian Gulf would exacerbate the existing pollution problems, while to import labour to the area would seem to be getting priorities wrong. Even Saudi Arabia, with its larger population, is planning to recruit 500,000 more foreign workers by 1980 to add to the existing foreign labour force of 314,000.

With serious planning Africa could become an ideal base for many Third World industries. Industrial pollution can be avoided by the considered location of key manufacturing and processing industries. Africa has an able, ready and willing labour force in every part of the continent and desperately needs to solve its growing unemployment problem. Moreover, Africa is blessed with limitless cheap hydro-electric power potential. The Inga project alone is capable of making the huge Republic of Zaire into an important industrial nation. Africa already has industries for semi-finished and finished products within its territories. For these industries to expand, money is required to buy plant and machinery. An Ivorian Ambassador attending the EEC-ACP meeting in Brussels in January 1975, quoted President Houphouet-Boigny as saying: 'The day when Africa is able to sell chocolate instead of cocoa, aluminium instead of bauxite, steel instead of iron ore, in short the day when Africa is able to transform on its own soil with its own people, its natural resources will be redeemed.'

The day that Felix Houphouet-Boigny was referring to is around the corner. Given financial and technical assistance from the Arab neighbours, Africans should be in a position to forge ahead to turn their poverty stricken areas into a paradise in which poverty, ignorance and disease will be no more than historical facts. Already Arab investment has started to flow into semi-Arab states like the Sudan and Mauritania, but perhaps the most hopeful sign for Black Africa has been a large-scale investment in the Republic of Guinea, a revolutionary state in West Africa, but one that is not entirely dominated by Islamic influence. The Arab experience there could well lead to new cooperative ventures elsewhere. The climax of Guinea's growing ties with the Arab world was the visit of Libya's Colonel Gaddafy to Conakry in November 1974. Economic, financial and cultural agreements were signed and a joint bank was set up. Saudi Arabia is participating in building a joint Guinea-Algeria oil refinery project. Kuwait made a loan to Guinea of 15 million dollars and Bahrain, Qatar and Egypt agreed to help Guinea's balance of payments difficulties. Egypt is participating in forestry development and establishing a paper mill.

The largest Arab project in Guinea is an alumina complex, which also involves constructing a new railway. Partners in the proposed Guinea-Arab Alumina Company are Kuwait, Libya, Egypt and Saudi Arabia. The bauxite reserves concerned total 500 million tons at Ayekoe, near to the Boke deposits currently being exported by an American consortium. The Arab company hopes to extract nine million tons annually, of which four million will be processed into alumina on the spot and the rest exported. The entire project requires investment of 400 million dollars, and it will eventually earn Guinea an estimated 250 million dollars a year.

8

The Arab Oil Countries and the African Development Banks

When I visited Saudi Arabia I had the privilege of speaking with distinguished persons who influence and manage that country's funds. I informed them that the majority of the African population was living below the poverty datum line and suggested to them that it would be a noble idea if the Arab states could invest some of their surplus funds in Africa. Their reply was that the blame is mutual. Some said that the African states have not as a group approached them for financial assistance but had preferred to complain through international forums. When Africa needs Arab support, Africa should not seek the assistance of a third party. Similarly when the Arab states want Africa to assist them they should approach them directly.

Most Arab leaders I met were opposed to aid to African states (or to any states for that matter) unless the money was to be spent on specific projects. Information available to them seemed to suggest that money given to some African states by certain donor countries had found its way into the pockets of senior civil servants and government ministers. The average citizen had thus not been able to benefit from these contributions. Except for such things as roads, hospitals and schools, money had often been spent on useless items such as skating rinks, swimming pools, Mercedes Benzes and Rolls Royces.

Some of these accusations may be valid but by and large they are isolated incidents which do not constitute the social and economic behaviour of the entire continent of Africa. During the last ten years the majority of African countries have done a lot in the economic field to alleviate the economic misery which has afflicted the continent for centuries. President Kaunda of Zambia had this to say:

We have achieved a measure of success in terms of building an economic infrastructure. First-class tarmac roads opening up almost all our provincial centres have been constructed. We have very good standard gravel roads joining every district with the rest of the country. We are now adding to our railway network by building the Tanzania-Zambia railway. We have good airstrips in each and every district, not to mention one of the finest international airports in Africa (Lusaka) and two others of international standards. In addition, our country can boast of innumerable first-class facilities. There are hundreds of thousands of primary school pupils, almost every district has a secondary school, and there are many teacher-training and technical colleges. Not least by any means there is, of course, the University of Zambia.

In so far as health facilities are concerned, we have a number of big hospitals in areas of large population concentration. We are also constructing large hospitals in each one of our rural provinces. Happily, every district can now boast of a standard rural hospital, or is at least in the process of having one constructed. This is to say nothing abour our 'under-five' clinics, ordinary clinics and dispensaries and, of course, the Zambia Flying Doctor Service, with its sister organisation, Medic-Air. In the social field, it is very encouraging to note that serious efforts have been made in the last few years to spread cultural and sport activities to rural areas. In many fields, culture and sport can and should be organised to play a great part in bringing out the dynamism of this young nation. All in all we have done extremely well. It is a record to be proud of, especially when one realises that all this has been accomplished in ten short years.

Let us now look at the institutions through which the Arab states can render financial economic assistance to their African brothers. Our survey will exclude UN specialised agencies such as the World Bank and the International Monetary Fund. As world organisations they have a global role to play. Here we are concerned with a specifically African problem.

State development banks

Some African countries have development banks. East Africa and Zambia are notable examples. The primary objective of these banks is to finance medium- and long-term projects. By definition commercial banks lend money on short-term projects, usually for a period not exceeding eighteen months, therefore projects which require loans for a longer period have to be financed by a development bank or any person or institution which is in a position to part with its funds for a longer period.

Under normal circumstances, projects financed by the development bank must be national in character. In other words, the benefit could either be in the form of providing employment to the community or in providing a service. For example, part of the funds of the Development Bank of Zambia were used to finance Mwembeshi Earth Station for Satellite Telecommunication. The initial effect on the Zambian communication system is that it will be relatively easier to get calls through to other countries and the quality of transmission will be as good as that obtained on local calls in most developed cities of the world. The inauguration of the Mwembeshi Earth Station took place on 21 October 1974.

The development banks are financed through the issue of stocks or bonds. The bonds ought to have a maturity value of at least five years. In emergency cases development banks sometimes obtain bridging finance from commercial banks. This only happens when for technical reasons the development bank is not able to lay its hands on some of its funds which may be lying somewhere in Europe or the US. As a rule the development bank tries to avoid borrowing money on short term, because of the high rate of interest charged by commercial banks.

In most cases development banks are constituted by Act of Parliament. They are not governed by company law, but for operational purposes they enjoy the rights and privileges of a limited company. They are considered to be artificial persons. They can sue and they can be sued just like an ordinary person. One of the basic differences between these banks and commercial banks is that the articles of a development bank cannot be varied except by a legally constituted body of Parliament or legislature.

Foreign participants in the development banks have objected

to what they have termed built-in interference by the legislature. They argue that since Parliament is supreme it can over-
rule the opinion of other shareholders under the pretence of
national interest. The Development Banks of Zambia and
Tanzania provide that the minister responsible for finance may
reverse any decision made by the board of the development bank.
The World Bank was critical of this provision. They argued that
the existence of this provision meant that the board would not
be an independent body, it would always be at the mercy of the
minister. The Zambian government explained that the
provision would not be used indiscriminately. All transactions
concluded in the normal course of business will be respected and
the minister responsible for finance will have no cause to interfere with the decision of the board. Obviously, if the board decided to give financial assistance to a government which was
hostile to Zambia, it is right and proper that the minister responsible for finance on behalf of the government should intervene.

Some students of African business management hold the
view that it is advantageous for foreign investors to own jointly
with the state shares in a development bank. Security of tenure
is advanced as one of the reasons.

In any country a government guarantee is as good as a gold
guarantee by the Bank of England. If a development bank is
owned and controlled by a state, the funds generated by the
bank will be utilised for the benefit of all its citizens. Where
they have development plans, projects on the priority list will
have precedence over other projects.

Most donor countries would like to be associated with specific
projects which they have financed. In other words, they would
like to have some influence in the planning and implementation
of the developmental budgets. This is natural and there is
nothing wrong with this intention. Last but not least, the risk
of nationalisation is minimised.

Some foreign investors are sceptical about development
banks organised and run by the states of Africa and other
developing countries. It is often argued that these banks
normally finance projects which have the highest risks. They
often undertake projects of an infrastructural nature. These are
projects which do not directly yield revenue and therefore as a
rule the return on such investments is very low. It takes at least

HE The Hon Mzee Jomo Kenyatta, GCH, MP
President of the Republic of Kenya

HH Sheikh Zaid bin Sultan Al Nahayyan
President of the United Arab Emirates

five years before a development bank would be in a position to pay modest dividends. In view of the uncertainty of income from capital invested in such a bank most entrepreneurs would prefer initially to offer a loan at a fixed rate of interest with a proviso that after a stipulated period the loan may be converted into shares. During this period, the investor would have ample time in which to observe whether the bank is viable.

It is alleged that state controlled development banks are inefficient because board members are not chosen according to their ability and experience in business management. All the board members are appointed by the state. They owe allegiance to the minister who appoints them. Most of them are said to be unable to tell the difference between a debit and a credit. Obviously, these accusations are made either by the people who have not had the opportunity to personally observe how Africans run their development banks, or by those who maliciously want to discredit the African states. Board members are appointed on merit. Some may not be bankers but they all have experience which enables them to execute the board's functions. Board members are drawn from various sections of the community. Some are teachers, lawyers, trade unionists, businessmen, farmers and others are political leaders at various levels. The board is designed to represent a cross-section of the entire nation.

It is contended that since board members are appointed by the state there is a tendency for the government to interfere in the board's decisions. The government will want to appoint party officials to senior management posts although they have no expertise for such technical jobs. Although the charter may provide that viable projects will have top priority, some people contend that the government can easily force the board to consider projects which are not viable and will not be beneficial to the community. They will be supported by the government for the simple reason that the applicants are politically acceptable and the board members are political appointees.

Again, the arguments are fallacious. Experience of the East African Development Bank proves the contrary. When the bank first opened its doors to the public in Kampala, Uganda, except for the general manager and his deputy, the top management was in the hands of expatriate professional men who had accumulated experience in banking. As time went on, Kenyan, Tanzanian and Ugandan nationals were able to learn the intricacies of banking. Most of these Africans were lawyers, engineers and accountants but they still had to acquire experience. After a reasonable period of training they were able to take over from their expatriate colleagues.

African governments establish development banks so that they can spread the economic benefits generated by the banks to a large section of the community. It would be self-defeating for the government to sponsor projects which would not benefit the community at large. On the contrary, the government will only intervene if there is reasonable cause to suspect that nepotism was being applied to loan applications. Again, experience in East Africa and Zambia shows that development banks are independent of government interference.

It has also been asserted that African politicians tend to mistrust professional advice genuinely given by expatriate personnel. They tend to associate them with the mentality of their former colonial masters who may have mistreated them. If one were to consider isolated cases one may possibly find such examples, but they are exceptions. On the contrary, African professionals often complain about the colonial hangover on the part of some politicians who often think that expatriate advice is always best. In practice one finds that professional advice is judged on its own merit. The source of advice is irrevelant: it can come from anybody. A good politician must always bear in mind that he remains responsible for any action he may wish to take. If the advice produces good results he will be congratulated for good service by his president. If on the other hand the advice so received makes him arrive at the wrong decision, he will have to accept full responsibility for the consequences.

It is not unusual to hear the so-called experts on African affairs say that money from the African development banks is handed out all too freely and easily. It is often said that a person who can neither read nor write could walk into a bank and ask for money in order to establish a clothing factory and within a matter of hours a cheque for the appropriate amount would be handed out to him. In other words, the critics allege that there is complete disregard for feasibility studies. Any person who has experience of any African development bank must have observed that the department dealing with feasibility studies is ranked number one in terms of importance. As a matter of fact, general managers are invariably groomed from this section. The department has at least two subsections, industrial and agricultural. Before any project is submitted to the board, it must be appraised. They must affix an estimated price tag and also indicate whether or not it is a viable project. To a very large extent board members are influenced by professional comments contained in the appraisal report.

To sum up: African development banks have been some of the most successful and important contributors to economic development in the countries in which they are established. They are free from political pressures but have the solid backing of their governments. Even in the case of a sudden change of government there is no disruption of their activities. They are staffed by experts who pay great attention to feasibility studies, and, most important, development banks always honour their commitments.

9

A Model for Afro-Arab Partnership

In the previous chapter we tried to correct some of the erroneous views shared by many people who are not familiar with the manner in which African states run their financial institutions. What we have said about the development banks is also true in many respects of the national commercial banks. In most Anglophone countries the basic difference between the two is that commercial banks come under company law, whereas development banks are created by an Act of Parliament.

Most of the financial and economic Arab advisers I had the opportunity to interview were of the opinion that Arab oil producing countries would rather give loans to African states than take equity participation in state owned companies. According to them, loans are more secure than shares. Apart from the fact that the value of shares fluctuates according to the trading operations of the enterprise, a shareholder does not normally ask for a guarantee. As a shareholder he takes a big risk. When the company makes a good profit he receives high dividends and when the company makes a loss he gets nothing and sometimes the value of his shares drops. This is the commercial risk, but there is also a political risk. The government may decide to nationalise the company and as a foreign shareholder you may not have recourse to arbitration.

The Arab oil countries would prefer to be bondholders rather than stockholders. When they lend money to an African state there will always be an agreement which sets out the terms of the loan. Except in very extreme circumstances, the borrower will offer some form of guarantee. When the agreement is concluded, the lender will be assured, within the agreed period, of receiving the principal sum plus interest. Under this arrangement the lender is in a position to forecast the income which will accrue to him in future with a certain amount of precision.

The Arab oil countries do not want to be passive investors. They are interested not only in income but also in the execution of the programmes. Under most company laws which exist in Africa, equity participation entitles one to have a say in the management of the company. Because the investor has no fixed income from his investment, he must be allowed to influence the affairs of the company so that it becomes profitable. A bondholder usually has a fixed income in the form of interest. Whether or not the company makes a profit he is assured of a fixed return on his investment. Since our Arab friends would like to participate in the management of the programmes or projects which they will help to finance, we shall have to strike a compromise. We shall deviate from the norm yet operate within the national laws of each and every African country. Our scheme will apply to both those countries who have development banks and those which own neither development banks nor national commercial banks.

At the very outset we would like to propose that for the scheme to be successful, Arab countries will have to deal with individual African countries and not as a group. The reason for this is very simple. Investment opportunities vary from one African country to another and, above all, they are at different levels of economic development. Some have a better infrastructure than others. Their propensity to spend is generally influenced by the nature of the infrastructure which exists in that country.

We would like the Arab investor to participate both in the policy making and management of the projects or programmes which are financed by them. This means that they will be represented on boards or councils and also on committees which award contracts to companies or firms engaged on carrying out projects.

We propose that the new scheme would operate as follows: whenever a financial and economic cooperation agreement has been concluded between an African state and an Arab oil state or financier, the two parties should form a council which will be charged with the responsibility of implementing the agreed objectives. The council would be perfectly legal in that it will represent the interests of the lenders and the borrowers. Since this will not be a board of representatives of shareholders which would require that the representation should be based on the share of the interest one has in a company, the council of lenders and borrowers should have parity representation. This is logical because the council will deal with one principal sum. For every debit there will be a corresponding credit. In countries that have development banks or financial institutions of similar character, such institutions would be permitted to submit their clients' projects to the council or board and the council would make funds available to the bank. The individuals, companies or firms would also be permitted to submit their projects to the board or council.

The financial and economic cooperation will be between the Arab investors and the government. The Arab investor may not necessarily be a government but the other party to the agreement should be a government because we want the agreement to be reinforced. A government guarantee is better than gold and diamonds. Most African heads of state are not keen on allowing individuals to borrow money from overseas because such funds may be redirected to numbered accounts in Zurich. President Kaunda of Zambia has this to say on the subject.

> Foreign capital is most welcome in Zambia provided it is made available, without strings, to the State or any other institution under it, for example, the Party, central government, local government, like the city municipal or rural councils, public corporations, trade unions, credit unions, thrift societies, etc. Individual Zambian businessmen will only be allowed to utilise new foreign capital in Zambia with the approval of the Government.

Another reason is that African countries want to borrow money to be used on projects and programmes which contribute to economic and social development. Such projects and programmes should benefit a greater population. The financial assistance from our Arab friends should complement the work done by the nationals of the recipient country. The African states should borrow money when they have satisfied themselves that their own resources cannot meet the new economic challenges. The borrowed money would be utilised generally on improvement of the economic situation of the country, in particular the introduction of the structures and factors whereby such improvement can be continued and extended by their own means.

It must be understood that we are talking of millions of dollars and not thousands of dollars and, therefore, it is imperative that there should be a proper accounting system. We should also remember that we are talking about medium- and long-term loans and that therefore the rate of interest and the duration of the loan agreement should be clearly stated. The loan agreement and the financial and economic cooperation would constitute two separate agreements. The former would be for a specific period and the latter for an indefinite period. The financial and economic agreement should merely state that the Arab country undertakes to provide funds within a period of six months from the date each contract has been concluded. In other words, money would be available within six months whenever a new project or programme which requires new money has been agreed upon by both parties. This procedure would be advantageous to both parties. The borrower would save on various commitment charges and also accumulated interest fees for the funds which are not being used. The lender might wish to invest in other ventures which yield a higher return. This money could be used by other developing countries which equally need financial assistance.

The financial and economic cooperation agreement should provide for the minimum aggregate amount and not the maximum. This is to allow for flexibility in the economic plans of the recipient countries and also the decline in the value of money.

Although the profit motive is not paramount as far as the Arab states are concerned, it is just, right and proper that they do not end up the losers in the final analysis. We recognise that there will be a general decline in the value of money and therefore, when the principal sum is finally repaid it will buy less goods than it would have done at the time the money changed hands. In view of this we do not recommend a fixed rate of interest. The London inter-bank rate should be the floor, with a maximum of one per cent above LIMBO.

Most of the projects to be financed will be of an infrastructural nature and therefore the rate of interest should not be above LIMBO.

The following projects should attract LIMBO rate of interest:

    i)   capital projects in the field of rural development
    ii)   projects related to tourism
    iii) economic and social infrastructure
    iv) schemes to improve the structure of agricultural production
    v)   industrial information and promotion schemes
    vi) marketing and sales promotion schemes
    vii) specific schemes designed to help small and medium sized national firms

In deciding the rate of interest to be charged, account would be taken of the nature of the project or programme. All commercial projects and productive capital projects in the industrial, oil and mining sectors should attract a higher rate of interest.

Although the agreement would be between the Arab state, individual or organisation, and an African state, the following should be eligible for financial and economic cooperation:

    i)   the state itself
    ii)   companies wholly owned by the state and companies in which the state has an interest
    iii) nationals
    iv) local authorities
    v)   state owned development banks
    vi) public and private companies working in the country concerned for the economic and social development of the population of that country

Both the donor and the recipient state would like to satisfy themselves that the proposed projects are either viable or are intended to accelerate the economic development of the country and therefore it will be necessary to prepare proper feasibility studies. The council or the board would appoint a competent person or persons to appraise projects or programmes. The appraisal will bring out certain facts which will assist the council or board in deciding whether or not the loan should be given to the applicant. The appraisal should ensure that the projects or programmes stem from economic plans of the recipient country and, in the case of industrial or commercial projects, the appraisal should ensure that, as far as possible, the methods selected constitute the most effective and profitable method of achieving the desired objectives.

In terms of technical know-how both the Arab states and the African states are in the process of developing. And, therefore, as regards operations financed by the Arabs, participation in tendering procedure for the award of contracts should be open on equal terms to all natural and legal persons of the contracting states. Employment in such projects would be open to all persons who are nationals of the contracting states.

The tenders should be advertised in reasonable time in all national papers of the contracting states and the person or persons charged with drawing up the tender procedure should ensure that there is no discriminatory practice or technical specification liable to stand in the way of participation on equal terms by all natural or legal persons of the contracting states.

Before any project is put to international tender, the two contracting parties must satisfy themselves that neither of them is competent enough to undertake such a project. In other words, any participation by a non-Arab country in contracts financed by the Arabs should have the concurrence of the Arab state or states. The basic exceptions to the rule would be for technical reasons, or to avoid delay in the completion of the project, or reduce transport costs, delivery dates or various transport difficulties. Participation by a third country might also be authorised where the project is a joint venture with another state that has also provided funds.

The management and maintenance of the work carried out in the context of financial and technical cooperation would be the sole responsibility of the recipient state. Self-reliance will be emphasised in most of the projects and programmes financed by the Arab states. Their assistance would be complementary to the efforts of the receiving state. It would not be right to expect Arab countries to provide us with shelters and at the same time to maintain these shelters in good condition. The financial and economic cooperation would not cover current administrative expenditure of the recipient country, but it should cover import costs, local expenditure and all operating expenses which are wholly and necessarily incurred for the execution of projects or programmes.

Loans to be awarded to small- and medium-sized national firms require special mention. Experience gained in several African countries tends to indicate that small- and medium-sized businesses are more likely to go bankrupt than big businesses. This is due to the fact that they have a very small working capital and the commercial banks are reluctant to come to their rescue. In view of this there must be some special guarantee accorded to them in respect of the loans given to small- and medium-sized national firms.

One of the best methods of financing small- and medium-sized national firms would be to finance them via public or semi-public financial bodies approved by the recipient country. Technically the loan agreement would be between the Arab state and the recipient country. Such public or semi-public financial bodies should undertake, on behalf of the small national firms, to provide the scope and nature of the projects to be financed; to state the amount of money required for the project. They should also undertake to provide any technical assistance required for the participation and management of the projects.

All the major projects under the proposed scheme should have a consultant. The contracting states should jointly select a consultant who should possess professional qualifications, relevant experience and independence. In no case should the contractor be authorised to carry on dual responsibilities. Some African countries have had the misfortune of being blessed with the rare professional advice from the World Bank to employ one person as both contractor and consultant engineer. The results have been disastrous to say the least. In matters of this nature, self-criticism is a rare commodity.

We have said that in order to promote employment opportunities in the contracting states, the national firms of the contracting states should be given preferential treatment over other companies; but their national firms should also meet strict professional standards. The tender selected must be the most advantageous, possess relevant experience and have technical know-how. Tenders allowing labour intensive methods should have an advantage over those not providing for a greater use of the physical and human resources. This would enable the African states to overcome or reduce the increasing unemployment caused by imported inflation.

This is a world of give and take and therefore it is just and natural that the Arab countries should also expect the recipient country to reciprocate in one form or another. The other contracting state should undertake to accord to the Arab state or states the most favoured nation treatment in respect of her imports and exports, provided that such treatment is not at variance with the provisions of agreements entered into with third states prior to the conclusion of agreements for financial and economic cooperation.

With their newly acquired wealth the Arab states will soon join the affluent club of industrial countries. The present geological data available does not indicate an abundance of mineral resources in Arab countries and therefore in the foreseeable future Arab countries are going to need raw materials from Africa. If the Arab states agree to work as a team with the African states, the Arab states will receive from the African states the unconditional most favoured nation treatment in respect of imports and exports.

We have already stated that this is a loan and not equity and therefore the African states should prove, beyond any reasonable doubt, that they will repay the principal sum plus interest within the agreed period. They should also state that, except for the reasons of serious economic disturbance or balance of payments problems, they will refrain from taking action in foreign transactions with regard to capital movements linked to investments which will be incompatible with their obligation under the agreement.

The proposed convention would be incomplete if it did not offer tax concessions to Arab investors. Most of the projects to be financed under this scheme would attract a concessionary rate of interest and therefore the Arabs would have a lower return on their investment. To compensate them against this financial loss, the African state concerned should exempt from tax any income earned by the Arab states, companies and firms. The exemption would apply to income accruing to them as a result of their involvement in the schemes or programmes being financed under financial and economic cooperation. Arab personnel should be allowed to bring in their personal effects duty free and their remunerations should be exempt from income tax, if they are not resident in the country for a period exceeding six months. The exemption from customs duty would not apply to goods and services acquired after they had been in the country for a period exceeding three months.

10

Investment Incentives in Modern Africa

If African states want to attract foreign capital, they must be prepared to offer attractive incentives to foreign investors. First and foremost, the commercial investor wants a higher return on his investment. If the investment is in the form of a loan, he would like to be assured that both parties to the loan agreement will observe the rules and regulations governing each and every transaction covered by the agreement. In particular, as a lender he would like at the end of the day to receive the principal sum plus interest.

The functions of investment have changed in the last three decades. Previously when people talked about capital movement they were referring to the transfer of cash and capital goods required for specific projects. Nowadays developing countries are in desperate need of foreign capital because foreign investment from industrial countries is often accompanied by the technological know-how which is in short supply. Technological know-how has become an integral part of most of the loans negotiated between the developing countries and the industrial countries. The only exception to this rule is the Eurodollar loans which have occupied a very important place in the European money market. It is generally believed that the Eurodollar market is the most important single financial development in Europe since the last war.

Before we look at specific investment incentives which are currently being offered by various African countries, we should indicate the type of incentives which will attract bigger investors to come to Africa.

Political climate is a very important factor to a person who wants to invest in a foreign country. If there is reasonable cause to suspect that there will be political instability in a given country the investor will, other things being equal, be reluctant to invest in that country. There is no guarantee on the part of the investor that with the change of government the *status quo* will be maintained. He often associates a change of government with a change for the worse rather than for the better. For the purpose of planning he would rather operate in a stable political system, in which a change of government does not necessarily mean a change of policy. He accepts the fact that governments come and go but the change of government should not necessarily mean a change in the fiscal laws affecting the business community.

A businessman, like the ordinary employee, is concerned about the 'take-home pay', the amount of money from his profits he would be allowed to repatriate to his country of domicile or permanent residence. This brings us to the question of the biggest incentive in business — exemption from direct and indirect taxes.

In order to develop industries such as farming and tourism the government should waive custom and excise charges on capital goods which are acquired for the purpose of being used in such industries. Companies or firms or individuals involved in farming or tourism should be accorded the following benefits:

Tax holiday

They should be given a tax holiday for a period not exceeding five years. This means that if they made a profit for tax purposes within the allowed period of grace that profit should not attract tax. If, on the other hand, they had assessed loss, that loss should be carried forward and set against future profits. The following two examples will explain the principle involved:

i) W & J Company was given a tax holiday for a period of five years from January 1975 to 31 December 1980. The profit and loss accounts for the period reflected the following balances:

January to December 1975	loss	$400,000
January to December 1976	loss	$200,000
January to December 1977	loss	$100,000
January to December 1978	loss	$ 50,000
January to December 1979	profit	$100,000
January to December 1980	profit	$400,000

January to December 1981	profit	$900,000

the company tax is 50 per cent

The tax assessment for this company will be as follows:

For the year ended 31 December 1975

profit as per tax computation	loss	$400,000
tax at 50 per cent		—
loss carried forward		$400,000

For the year ended 31 December 1976

assessed loss for 1975	$400,000
profit as per tax computation 1976	$200,000
loss carried forward	$600,000

For the year ended 31 December 1977

loss brought forward	$600,000
profit as for tax computation 1977 loss	$100,000
loss carried forward	$700,000

For the year ended 31 December 1978

loss brought forward	$700,000
profit as per tax computation 1978 loss	$ 50,000
loss carried forward	$750,000

For the year ended 31 December 1979

loss brought forward	$750,000
profit as per tax computation 1979	$100,000
loss carried forward	$650,000

For the year ended 31 December 1980

loss brought forward	$650,000
profit as per tax computation 1980	$400,000
loss carried forward	$250,000

For the year ended 31 December 1981

loss brought forward	$250,000
Profit as per tax computation 1981	$900,000
Profit	$650,000
Tax payable (50 per cent of $650,000)	$325,000

ii) M & S Company was given a tax holiday for a period of three years from January 1975 to December 1977. The profit and loss account for the period reflected the following balances:

January to December 1975	loss	$100,000
January to December 1976	profit	$200,000
January to December 1977	profit	$300,000
January to December 1978	profit	$350,000

The tax assessment for M & S Company will be as follows:

Assessed loss for 1975	$100,000
tax	$ —
loss carried forward	$100,000
Profit for 1976	$200,000
less loss brought forward	$100,000
Profit	$100,000

Tax payable nil because of tax holiday

Assessed profit for 1977 $300,000

Tax payable nil because of tax holiday

Assessed profit for 1978 $350,000

Tax payable (50 per cent of $350,000) $175,000

Capital expenditure relief

Most African countries have given top priority to agriculture.

HE General Gaafar Mohamed Numeiri
President of Democratic Republic of Sudan

HH Sheikh Rashid bin Said al Maktoum
Vice President of the United Arab Emirates and
Ruler of Dubai

The East African Community has a common income tax law with very generous provisions for farmers. Their law provides for accelerated depreciation for plant, buildings, equipment, dams and other capital works. If a person acquires plant and equipment worth 100,000 dollars he would be granted 60,000 dollars during the first year as tax allowances. Of course he must prove that it was wholly and exclusively used in the production of income from farming. The allowances would be calculated as follows:

1st year

Cost of machinery		$100,000
less: 20 per cent initial allowance	$20,000	
40 per cent wear and tear	$40,000	$60,000
		$40,000

60,000 dollars will be deducted from income as capital expenditure wholly and exclusively incurred in the production of income. The initial allowance is not included in arriving at the written down value and therefore the written down value in our example above will be the cost of the machinery less allowances for wear and tear which gives us 60,000 dollars. In the following year the wear and tear will be calculated as follows:

written down value	$60,000
less 40 per cent wear and tear	$24,000
	$36,000

The above is an example of an accelerated depreciation allowance. It has been given this name because it deviates from the standard procedure which does not allow for a higher rate of depreciation allowance for capital expenditure.

Normally accelerated depreciation allowances attract people who are already in the industry. If you want to attract new blood into the system you need different kinds of incentives, ones which will enable new investors to compete effectively with those who have been in the industry without appearing to favour the new arrival. To do this you need to decide on a base year. Then you can say that any capital expenditure wholly and exclusively incurred in the production of income from the base year will be allowed in full in the year it is incurred.

We have to admit that allowing in full any capital expenditure in the year it is incurred is a complete departure from the normal commercial accounting procedure. In fact what we are doing is to treat capital expenditure as though it were revenue expenditure. This of course simplifies the accounting system from the income tax point of view.

The reader may begin to think that if tax authorities allowed him to write off capital expenditure in the year it is incurred it will no longer be necessary for him to prepare proper books of accounts. It is regretted that this type of reasoning is misleading. The farmer still needs to prepare accounts in accordance with the accepted commercial accounting principles in order for him to know whether or not he is making a profit. If he wants to obtain a loan from financial institutions they will require proper books of accounts.

Surprisingly enough the income tax authorities would insist on a proper breakdown of various items in the accounts. The reader might have observed that we have always qualified the expenditure with the words 'wholly and exclusively'. For any expenditure to be allowed it must be wholly and exclusively incurred in the production of income. The basic rule to apply if one wants to know whether or not the expenditure is wholly and exclusively incurred in the production of income is to try to establish a relationship between the expenditure being claimed and the revenue it is supposed to have generated. This rule only applies if the law under which you are claiming this expenditure does not specifically prohibit that expenditure. Let us illustrate this by an example:

P & J Company

P & J Company starts farming in January 1975. During the year it earns income of $100,000 and incurs the following expenditure: Seeds $1,000, fertilisers $10,000, wages $20,000, tractors $5,000, lorries $5,000, oil $2,000, repairs for tractors and lorries $3,000, irrigation $10,000, entertainments $5,000. We assume that the tax law does not allow for entertainment expenditure. We also assume that the law permits that capital expenditure wholly and exclusively incurred in the production of income should be allowed in the year in which it is incurred. The accounts will be prepared as follows:

P & J Company

Sales		$100,000
Less Expenses		
Cost of seeds	$1,000	
Fertiliser	$10,000	
Wages	$20,000	
Oil	$2,000	
Repairs	$3,000	
Irrigation	$10,000	
Entertainment	$5,000	
Depreciation of 20 per cent		
Tractors	$1,000	
Lorries	$1,000	$53,000
Profit as per accounts		$47,000

Income Tax Computation		
Profit as per accounts		$47,000
add depreciation		
tractors	$1,000	
entertainment	$5,000	
lorries	$1,000	$7,000
		$54,000
Less		
Capital expenditure		
tractors	$5,000	
lorries	$5,000	$10,000
Profit for tax purposes		$44,000

Some income tax laws do not allow capital expenditure incurred on furnished accommodation for both the owner and his management staff. In most African countries urban areas are becoming more and more overpopulated and therefore to encourage people to go back to the land we have to create job opportunities in the rural areas. This can be achieved by treating investors who are prepared to develop our rural areas more favourably than those who want to set up factories in urban areas. In the case of a commercial farmer who decides to establish a farm in a rural area the tax law should grant him exemption on furnished accommodation both for himself and his staff. The expenditure should be allowed in full in the year it is incurred.

Import licences

Capital goods are not readily available in most African countries and therefore in countries which operate import licences the farmer should be granted licences related to agricultural equipment promptly. Rain in Africa is seasonal and therefore any delay in the granting of licences could mean a substantial decline in the agricultural output.

Insurance policies

A foreign investor like any wage earner would like to prepare for a rainy day and therefore as a foreigner he would like to contribute to various saving schemes operating in his country of residence. If he takes up an annuity or if he contributes to an internationally recognised insurance company or companies, his yearly premiums should be allowed in full for tax purposes as a deduction from his income.

Minimum guaranteed prices

Let us take tourism as an example of how minimum prices may be introduced. Having agreed on the standard of the hotels to be constructed, the government and the hotel industry should agree on the minimum charges for the room and other services. This is essential for an industry which has to budget for a minimum period of five years. Naturally the government would also like to know the number of people who are likely to be employed by the industry.

Farmers would also like to know how much the consumer is likely to pay for their products. In order to encourage the production of certain selected cash crops, the government should guarantee minimum prices for all agricultural commodities grown under specific schemes authorised by the government. As an additional incentive, the government should set up marketing boards to ensure that all products grown under special schemes are either bought by the government at the minimum guaranteed prices or are sold to the public at prices not less than the minimum.

Transfer of profits

Some countries insist that a foreign company can only transfer profits earned in convertible currencies. Of course the intention is to maximise their foreign exchange earnings. But such an exchange regulation does not stand a rational test. Some firms and organisations are there solely to provide goods and services to the nationals of those states and therefore it is illogical for the government to expect them to earn their receipts in foreign currencies. In the case of a farmer, he would be expected to produce crops which are mainly marketable in foreign countries. If the African states are really genuine about their desire to grow more food then they must attract foreign investors by allowing them to transfer part of the net profits earned within their territories. If farmers are allowed to transfer some of the profits earned to their countries of residence they are likely to show a profit. In Zambia, ever since farmers were allowed to remit overseas 10 per cent of their net profit even the companies which were formerly making losses have turned into profit making enterprises.

Tax sparing credits

When African countries negotiate double taxation conventions with industrial countries they should insist on including a clause relating to tax sparing credit. This clause would provide that any natural or legal person who is exempt from tax in one of the contracting states should be exempt from tax in the other contracting state. This means that if a company performs duties which assist in the economic development of a country and the income earned is exempt under the tax law of that developing country the industrial country should not tax that income; in other words, the industrial country should assume tax as having been paid in the developing country. Such a provision would encourage big enterprises to invest in developing countries. For reasons known to themselves, the US government has repeatedly rejected the tax sparing credit clause in their double taxation convention with the countries of the Third World.

Since most of the investment in government controlled companies will be in the form of loans, it is necessary for the African states to offer special tax incentives to this type of investment. The tax sparing credit clause should particularly apply to income from loan capital.

Taxation of interest

In most double taxation conventions, interest is the most difficult income to tax. There are no clear-cut rules as to who should tax interest from capital. Where the borrower and the lender are resident for tax purposes in the same country the provisions of the internal law apply. In the Anglophone countries, the borrowers will treat interest as an expenditure wholly and exclusively incurred in the production of income and the lender will treat it as income and pay appropriate tax if any. If the lender and the borrower are resident in two different states then it becomes difficult to decide the source of interest. One school of thought believes that interest arises in the country in which the loan is being utilised and the other school maintains that interest arises from the country of residence of the owner of capital. Both sides have very strong and rational arguments. The country of residence for the lender argues that if they did not sacrifice consumption, in order to save, the country of residence for the borrower would not have had the opportunity to utilise that capital. The country of residence for the borrower contends that it is entitled to tax interest because the loan has been utilised within its boundaries and therefore the source of interest is in that country.

As we have said before, African states need foreign capital. They cannot have their cake and eat it. There must be room for sacrifice and therefore as far as interest is concerned they must be the losers. They should make provision in their tax laws for the exemption of tax on interest earned by a person or persons who are non-resident in their countries and have loaned money to a person or persons carrying on business in that country. As a matter of fact, most African states exempt interest earned by UN agencies such as the World Bank and International Monetary Fund, and other organisations, i.e. KFW (wholly-owned financial organisations of West Germany) and EXIM Bank (a wholly-owned financial organisation of the US). Hence, we are merely requesting the African states to offer the same preferential treatment to other big investors who are also contributing to the economic development of Africa.

Investment incentives are by nature and definition discriminatory. Unless someone is able to offer something extraordinary it is not necessary to attract him. You must let him compete with the rest in order to earn his living. A tip to a waiter implies that the waiter has rendered services over and above what he is required to do in the performance of his duties. Similarly, we want to offer incentives to foreign investors because we sincerely believe that they will either perform better or they will appreciably contribute to the increase of our national product.

Concessions in manufacturing

In the preceding paragraphs we have talked about the farming and tourist industries. These are not the only industries which operate in African countries. Most of the industries of Europe have their replica in Africa. But to many African states these two are the main sources of revenue.

In order to encourage new industries from foreign countries some African countries have set up what they call a 'Pioneer Industries Act'. Zambia is a good example. The main provision of this Act is a tax holiday usually for a period not exceeding five years. The length of tax exemption is decided upon on the basis of the capital to be invested in business. The higher the capital the longer the period of exemption. There is also a minimum amount of capital to be invested in business in order to qualify for a tax holiday. For a business to qualify for a tax holiday status, the investor should go into either a unique venture or a business which in the opinion of the government will greatly accelerate the rate of economic development of the country. The former is very difficult to establish, the latter is often subject to abuse by corrupt officials and government ministers. What is the yardstick for deciding that a particular business is contributing more than others towards the economic development of the country?

Taxation of personal income

So far we have made recommendations in respect of incentives to be given only to the owners of capital and not to their top managers, who are in short supply. We have said that foreign investment is often accompanied by technological know-how. We now want to consider the type of incentives to be given to these technocrats. Our remarks will be confined to 'guest' technocrats and not to the nationals of a state recruiting foreign experts.

When a top-class technocrat looks in the advertisement section of *The Times* newspaper in London for jobs being advertised in African countries, his main interest will be in the take-home pay, including such benefits as pension and gratuities. Unless these benefits are attractive he would not bother to apply for the jobs being advertised.

If an African government has a special scheme which they think is essential for their economic development and if foreign capital and foreign expertise are required to implement that scheme, it is necessary to make a package deal which will include incentives to expatriate employees. It is important to note that here we are talking about experts of international standing and not ordinary guest workers with professional qualifications. They should be allowed tax free emoluments for a maximum period of two years. The term emolument includes wages, salaries, overtime, gratuities and other benefits whether or not they are capable of being realised into money. They should receive 50 per cent gratuity of their total salaries or wages as the case may be.

In some countries the expenses incurred in travelling from one's residence to one's working place are disallowed by tax authorities as being private or domestic expenditure. It has been argued that the individual acts according to his own volition as to where he is going to stay. Some legal brains have gone as far as saying that if he wanted to be near his place of work he could either sleep under a tree or in his car. This argument is theoretical. In the first place it is very risky to sleep under a tree and above all man is by nature a social animal and would like to be with his fellow human beings. In the case of an expatriate he may be allocated a company house which is far from his place of work. If the company provides him with transport the tax authorities will construe it as income and tax him accordingly. In our view the income tax law should allow this type of expenditure as an expenditure wholly and exclusively incurred in the production of income.

Tax avoidance by non-distribution of dividends

Tax avoidance differs from tax evasion in that tax evasion is illegal and tax avoidance is legal. For example, when a taxpayer deliberately underestimates his stock in trade he is trying to evade tax by carrying out an illegal transaction. On the other hand, a taxpayer is legally entitled to arrange his tax affairs within the law in such a way that his liability to tax is substantially reduced or wiped out. Tax avoidance involves taking advantage of the loopholes in the tax legislation.

Some companies try to avoid tax by non-distribution of dividends. This normally happens when the law provides that the company will be treated as a person and as such become taxable on any income accruing to it. When the company declares the dividends such dividends will be treated as income in the hands of the recipients and appropriate tax will be levied on the person receiving the dividends. If tax is being charged on the profits of the company and dividends are taxed in the hands of the recipient or recipients then it is true to say that income produced by that company is being taxed twice.

If it is a family company or if the company is owned and controlled by a handful of persons who have close ties, they can reduce their tax liability by non-distribution of dividends. The example below illustrates this point:

PJK Company makes a profit of $20,000. The two directors who own and manage the company receive $8,000 each as remuneration for the services rendered to the company. The company tax is 40 per cent and the rate of tax for individuals is 50 per cent.

If the company decides to declare dividends, the two directors will be assessed as follows:

Profit as per accounts	$20,000
Company tax 40 per cent	$8,000
Amount available for distribution as dividends	$12,000
Dividends to Shareholder A	$6,000
Dividends to Shareholder B	$6,000

	Shareholder A	Shareholder B
Salary	$8,000	$8,000
Dividend	$6,000	$6,000
Total Income	$14,000	$14,000
Tax 50 per cent of $14,000	$7,000	$7,000

If the company decided not to declare a dividend the executive directors only pay tax on their salaries which will be $4,000. The directors can only succeed in avoiding tax by non-distribution of dividends if the legislation is silent on this matter. To prevent people from taking advantage of this tax loophole the tax law should provide that where a person charged with the duty of assessing and collecting taxes determines that a company has not distributed to its shareholders as dividends, within a reasonable time after the end of any year for which the accounts have been prepared, such part of its income as could be so distributed without detriment to the company business, he may treat such income as having been distributed. The amount treated as having been distributed shall be treated as having been received by the shareholders and the persons concerned shall be assessable accordingly.

We have just stated a general rule. There are several cases in which the rule may be waived or relaxed. The company may decide not to declare dividends because such action may be detrimental to the company's business. The company may not declare dividends under the following circumstances:

a)   If a company has a large overdraft (a bank loan whereby a person is allowed to overdraw his account).

b)   If a company has a loan from a person who does not have an interest in that company and does not directly or indirectly control it and the condition of the loan is that no dividends shall be declared until the full amount of the loan has been repaid.

c)   In the case of bad subsequent years the company may find it difficult to declare dividends without causing injury to business. This would be particularly relevant to farming. A good year may be followed by a bad year because of changes in the amount of rainfall. This is also true of exports which are subject to fluctuation in the international market, e.g. the price of copper was about £1,000 at the beginning of 1974 and by the end of the same year the price was down to £540 per metric ton.

d)   If the company wants to plough back the profits in order to buy capital equipment or other expenses related to the expansion of the business.

e)   General world economic and monetary trends such as depression, devaluation and also government fiscal and monetary policies.

f)   *Force majeure.*

For obvious reasons the tax avoidance provisions will also not apply in the following cases:

a)   where the ordinary share capital of the company may be bought or sold on a stock exchange;

b)   where the company is controlled by a company to which (a) above applies;

c)   where the company is controlled directly or indirectly by the government;

d)   where the company's assessable income plus non-
chargeable income is less than $2,000 (to avoid
unnecessary administrative work).

The provisions should be applied only where it is considered
that an amount has not been distributed with a view to the
avoidance or reduction of tax.

11

Incentives in the Mining Industry

Mining is one of the most lucrative industries in Africa. Despite the occasional fluctuations in the price of minerals in the international market, minerals still offer a better yield on the capital invested than other industries. Other things being equal, the investor expects a good return on his investment and the government is also assured of reasonable revenue in the form of taxes. Loss only occurs if the management is inefficient or the planning is too ambitious. A foreign investor who is looking for a quick return on his investment is advised to invest in a mining venture.

Capital gravitates where the return is good and prospects of its appropriation are less. If the developing countries of Africa are in search of foreign capital they must ensure its safe return to the base with a reasonable return. They should not be greedy by enacting fiscal laws which enable them to reap everything where they did not sow. The fiscal laws should be such that both the state and the investor benefit from the income produced by the capital applied to a given industry.

At the risk of repetition, we have to state once more that the primary objective of every commercial investor is to make a profit. Some scholars have eloquently argued the point that businesses are there to provide goods and services to the community both within and outside the areas in which they are located. We contend that no business can survive for a long time unless it is operating above the break-even point. In view of this, developing countries of Africa will attract foreign investment only if they offer both incentives which will guarantee good return on capital invested and unqualified assurances that both capital and income from it will be remitted to the country or countries where the capital originated. I would like to spell out some fairly extensive alterations to the present taxation of mining companies in Africa.

Capital allowance (based on the life of a mine)

It is fashionable nowadays to give capital allowance to mining companies based on the life of a mine. The capital expenditure to be allowed would be ascertained as follows:

a) For the first relevant accounting period, the quotient resulting from the total capital expenditure up to the end of that year, less any recoveries from capital expenditure, divided by five;

b) For the second, third and fourth accounting years, the quotient resulting from the sum of unredeemed capital expenditure at the commencement of the accounting year, plus the amount of capital expenditure incurred during that year, less any rebates, recoveries or returns from capital expenditure, divided by four, three or two respectively;

c) For any accounting year subsequent to the fourth, the sum of the unredeemed capital expenditure at the commencement of the accounting, plus the amount of capital expenditure incurred during that year less any recoveries from capital expenditure.

In mining operations capital expenditure includes expenditure on:

a) building, works, railway lines or equipment, including any premium or consideration in the nature of a premium paid for the use of buildings, works, railway lines, equipment or land;

b) shaft sinking;

c) the purchase of or on the payment of a premium for the use of, any patent, design, trade mark, process or other expenditure of similar nature;

d) preliminary surveys, boreholes, development or management, including any interest on loans used for mining purposes;

e) shaft-sinking, including expenditure on sumps, pump chambers, stations and ore bins accessory to a shaft.

The capital allowance based on the life of a mine does not provide adequate incentives to the investor. It is often based on the unwarranted assumption that the money invested in business is in the form of equity and not loan capital. Mining operations require large sums of money which are often loaned on a short-term basis, and therefore in addition to the tax to be paid to the state the company is duty bound to make provisions for the repayment of the loan plus interest.

Capital expenditure to be allowed in full

In those African countries where mining is not yet being run on a large scale the risk is greater. Therefore to attract a large amount of foreign capital a new mine should be given a tax holiday of at least four years and thereafter the recommendation in the following paragraphs should be applied. The capital expenditure wholly and exclusively incurred for purposes of operating a mine should be allowed in the year in which it is incurred. This could be done as follows:
  a) for the year, the total capital expenditure incurred up to the end of that year less any recoveries from capital expenditure;
  b) for subsequent years, the amount of capital expenditure incurred during a charge year less any recoveries from capital expenditure.

In addition to the expenditure being allowed in the year in which it is incurred, there should be an investment allowance of 10 per cent of capital expenditure incurred, i.e. if a person carrying on the business of mining incurs £900,000 capital expenditure for a given financial year, for tax purposes he should be given the following allowances: £900,000 capital expenditure and £90,000 investment allowance.

Deductions for prospecting and exploration operations

Prospecting and exploration is a prerequisite to any mining operation. As a rule during the period of prospecting and exploration people carrying on such activities earn no income at all, and therefore for a state to encourage them to carry on such activities it should offer them some incentives. It is common practice for the states to allow losses incurred in the prospecting and exploration activities to be set against future profits of the mine. Some states disregard prospecting and exploration expenditure incurred in areas where no minerals have been found. Both practices are inadequate and unsatisfactory. We now wish to recommend incentives which are likely to attract foreign capital.

For a company carrying on mining operations in the same country any expenditure incurred by that company on prospecting and exploration in any given year should be allowed as a deduction against income earned from mining operation. If a company other than a company carrying on mining operations incurs expenditure on prospecting or exploration, it should be allowed to elect to renounce such deduction in favour of its shareholders or partners. In such a case the deduction should be allowed to such shareholders in proportion to their investment in the company.

The problem of tax avoidance

The right to renounce deduction in favour of shareholders or partners raises tax avoidance problems. It may encourage persons making large profits to buy shares in prospecting and exploration companies so as to take advantage of tax provision which allows such companies to renounce their losses in favour of shareholders. In order to prevent such companies from trafficking in assessed losses, the fiscal law should authorise persons responsible for the assessment of tax to disregard such transactions. The law should provide that where, in the opinion of tax officers, any change in the shareholding of the company or partnership has been effected by any person solely or mainly for the purpose of utilising any loss incurred by the company in order to avoid tax liability, the loss incurred by the company carrying on the business of prospecting and exploration prior to the charge year in which the change in the shareholding took place shall not be allowed as a deduction against the income of new shareholders.

Apart from a specific provision designed to prevent companies from trafficking in assessed losses, the fiscal law should also have a general provision to counteract transactions designed to avoid liability to tax. The fiscal law should provide that where, in the opinion of persons charged with the responsibility of assessing and collecting taxes, there is a reasonable ground to believe that the main purpose, or one of the main purposes for which any transaction was effected was the avoidance or reduction of liability to tax for any charge

HE Dr Mwalimu Julius Kambarage Nyerere
President of the United Republic of Tanzania

HE Lt Gen Olusegun Obasanjo
Head of Federal Military Government,
Commander-in-Chief of Armed Forces of Nigeria

year, the tax officer should make appropriate adjustment to counteract the avoidance or reduction of liability to tax.

Some foreign tax experts working in Africa have recommended that where a mining company ceases operating and has accumulated losses, the company should be reassessed to enable it to recoup some of the taxes paid in the previous years. They suggest that to achieve this objective the fiscal law should provide for the cessation operations due to expiration of the life of a mine, or for any other reason acceptable to tax authorities. If the person involved in such a mining operation so elects within one year of the end of the charge year during which operation ceased, the deductions from his income should be ascertained as follows:

a) the balance of the unredeemed capital expenditure at the beginning of the fifth year preceding the year of cessation plus capital expenditure incurred during the last tax years in which the mine operated, including the year of cessation, less recoveries from capital expenditure from the disposal of all assets ranking for redemption, is divided by six and;

b) The amount so arrived at shall be the deduction of the last six tax years including the year of cessation.

This proposal would, however, certainly disrupt African development plans. The countries concerned would be called upon to effect refunds for tax paid· in prior years. Such a proposal is not an incentive, it is ill-conceived and would be a glaring example of mismanagement on the part of the government concerned. Good investors who want to make a good profit and in the process participate in the development of the economy would not offer such a provision as a condition for their investment.

It is important to note that capital expenditure of the mining companies should only be allowed in respect of income from mining operations. The only exception to this rule is the expenditure incurred by a company carrying on the business of prospecting and exploration which may be deducted from income other than income from mining operations.

12
Guarantees Against Nationalisation and Compensation Agreements

Businesses, like governments, have short- and long-term plans. Business prudence demands that companies should prepare budgets which will indicate the projected profits or losses within a specified period. Such budgets play important roles in their decision making as to whether or not they should remain in that type of business or move on to new pastures. It is often asserted that business budgets in Africa contain one unknown factor, namely nationalisation. Businesses do not often know how to account for it. The host government often decides to nationalise a company without paying due regard to the commitment of the company. Even where compensation is made, the amount representing compensation is often less than the contractual obligation of the company.

Because of the large sums of money involved, mining companies are particularly sensitive to the threat of nationalisation. We would like to make some recommendations which may be advantageous to both the foreign investor and the host government.

In the chapter dealing with new forms of investment appropriate to developing countries of Africa, we have recommended a council consisting of government representatives of the creditors. We have also recommended that there should be a binding agreement between the state and the person or persons lending money. To avoid unnecessary anxiety on the part of the investor who decides to take equity participation, the agreement should provide for a minimum number of years within which the foreign company would be allowed to operate without due government intervention. In the event of a government takeover, the agreement should provide the formula for compensation. They could either agree on a book value or market value basis.

Assessing market value in Africa poses some insurmountable

problems. Mines in Africa are often in monopolistic positions and therefore there is no basis for comparison. Even with a mineral like copper in Zambia and Zaire, the unit costs in each country are different and the break-even points are different. Therefore at the time of sale of a mine there is often no yardstick. The price is simply negotiated and often has no bearing on either the book value or the market value. Sometimes it is a compromise between the two. We are unable to recommend a formula which would be acceptable to both parties, but we strongly recommend that to avoid hard feelings during the time of the takeover, the agreement should spell out in clear terms how the compensation is going to be arrived at. To illustrate this point, let us look at the acquisition of 51 per cent interest by the Zambian government in the copper mining industry.

Mining: How Zambia took control

Mining in Zambia has been dominated from the turn of the century by two conglomerates, the Anglo American Corporation and Amax. The history of Zambia is incomplete without mentioning the contribution these two giant companies have made to the country's development. Indeed, all political, social and economic activities were dominated to a very large extent by developments on the Copperbelt where a large working force from all parts of Zambia was concentrated.

Mining in Zambia by local inhabitants goes as far back as 1898 but it was not until around 1903 that commercial mining started on a large scale. Amax and Anglo took out large prospecting areas of what is now called the Copperbelt, for their own need and future activities. The Copperbelt was considered the most viable part of the country. The rock formation indicated a large presence of various minerals, and it was therefore not strange that these two mining companies chose the area in question. This is not a history of the mining industry, but I think it is important to understand the background to the various economic events which have taken place since Independence.

The most dramatic changes in the Zambian mining industry came in August 1969, when President Kaunda announced his government's intention to take a 51 per cent majority interest in the mines owned by the Anglo and Amax group.

Negotiations were protracted and at times sticky, but they were concluded in December of the same year and on 1 January 1970, the changes were effected and a newly structured mining industry was born. The two mining companies were fully compensated for the government takeover of 51 per cent. The compensation was based on the audited accounts as at 31 December 1969, based on book value. RST (Roan Selection Trust) received 117.8 million dollars and Zambian Anglo American received 178.7 million dollars. In settlement of these debts the state agreed to pay annual amounts of 19 million dollars to Anglo and 15 million dollars to RST even if the price of copper fell to zero.

Basically, the Anglo American group of mines was reconstituted to form a new division called NCCM Limited (Nchanga Consolidated Copper Mines Limited) and the Amax group of mines were reconstituted to form a new division called RCM Limited (Roan Consolidated Mines Limited). The government held its 51 per cent in both companies through a new holding company called Mindeco Limited (The Mining Development Corporation) which was 100 per cent owned by the government of Zambia. Mindeco in turn was owned by the government through another 100 per cent corporation called Zambian Industrial and Mining Corporation (Zimco Limited) which was the supreme holding body of all government investments in the private sector. Its chairman was the President.

Under the 1970 scheme of arrangements the government realised that in order to effect the changes as quickly as possible and in order to minimise dislocations and disruptions, it was important to retain existing services provided by the Anglo and Amax groups in the form of management, financial, technical and marketing expertise. These arrangements were entered into for a period of eight years for one group and ten years for the other. The government paid management and marketing fees for the services provided and this is a situation which continued until August 1973.

It was not for lack of foresight and understanding that the government accepted an agreement whose provisions were not in harmony with the economic aspirations of the Zambian people. But as the Chairman of Finance, Sub-Committee of the

United National Independence Party, Mr H. Mulemba, put it: 'The government did not have the immediate cash to pay for a 51 per cent shareholding in the two mining companies, and therefore in the interest of the Zambian economy it had to accommodate the interest of foreign investors.' The following were some of the objectionable provisions:

Until all the outstanding bonds were redeemed:

a) the government would not enact tax legislation which would affect the two mining companies;

b) irrespective of the state of the economy the two mining companies were allowed to remit all dividends due and payable to foreign shareholders;

c) under the agreement the two mining companies had wide powers of veto; unless the minority shareholders supported a board decision, such a decision would not be implemented, irrespective of whether or not it was economically sound or it was in the interest of the Zambian economy as a whole;

d) the minority shareholders had a complete monopoly of the management and sales contracts. The government was a passive investor.

The Zambian government soon felt that the minority shareholders were not playing a fair game. Even during 1970 and 1971 when the price of copper was very low and the cave-in at Mufulira Mine caused a disaster which claimed twenty-nine lives and reduced copper production, both Anglo and Amax took out all the profits to which they were entitled. Nothing was left for reinvestment; instead they resorted to borrowing in the European market. The rates of interest for Eurodollars borrowed were as high as 13 per cent. When the time was ripe and after a careful and critical examination of the limitations placed on the government by the management and consultancy agreements, the government once again decided to invoke a series of new measures which changed further the structure of the mining industry. Thus in August 1973, President Kaunda announced that the government would terminate, with immediate effect, management, marketing and consultancy services with both Anglo and Amax.

In order to terminate the agreements the government was required under the agreement to redeem Zimco Bonds, which it did. As part of the cleaning up operation, the government decided that Mindeco would no longer be a holding company for RCM and NCCM and was instead designated as a mining house on its own, at par with RCM and NCCM. Mindeco was given the responsibility of developing new mines and to spearhead new development on behalf of the government. Its area of responsibility included the control of Maamba collieries and the exploration of small mines like Kafabu emeralds, Chifumpa, Lochinvar, etc.

For Zambia, copper is a strategic raw material and the government could not leave the marketing of such a commodity indefinitely in the hands of foreign investors. As part of the new measures the government formed a new Metal Marketing Corporation (Memaco), wholly owned by the government, to take over the responsibility of marketing Zambian metals throughout the world. Its first task was to take over from the existing marketing companies of Anglo American Corporation and Amax, i.e. Anmercosa Sales Limited and Ametalco Limited, whose base of operations was in London.

Traditionally Anglo had channelled products from its mines through its own marketing subsidiary, Anmercosa Sales Limited, while Amax channelled all products from its mines through its own subsidiary, Ametalco Limited. This was the situation pertaining at the time of the 1973 announcement. In addition to the operations in the London offices, these companies had a series of sub-agency networks throughout the world and especially in those countries where Zambian metals were sold, but which were difficult to service from London. The system of sub-agents, therefore, reflects the historic pattern of the mining industry in Zambia and thus there was little consultation between the two companies when it came to marketing policy. For these services the Zambian government paid 75 per cent of the total turnover and 2 per cent of profits after mineral tax but before income tax for management and consultancy services. For sales contracts they received 0.75 per cent of total turnover. The total amount paid to them was colossal when one takes into account that the combined gross turnover of the two mining companies was well over 500 million dollars per year. In 1974 Anglo estimated her revenue from these services to be K11.58 million and RCM estimated her revenue to be K8 million.

The management, consultancy and sales agreements have now been terminated. The Anglo American Corporation and the RST have been paid handsome compensation. The Metal Marketing Corporation has formed a new UK subsidiary called Memaco Services Limited, which is responsible for the servicing of all contracts with European manufacturers on behalf of the holding company in Lusaka. Memaco Services Limited was formed out of a desire to maintain quick efficient links with the market and the customer as well as to provide on the spot all necessary information and services which the two former marketing companies provided to the industry in general and to the customer in particular. Due to communications and other difficulties, it was not possible to handle the work in Zambia. All in all, Memaco Limited is responsible for the disposal of about 700,000 metric tons of copper, about 800,000 tons of lead and zinc, 2,000 tons of cobalt as well as ancillary products like gold, silver and selenium. Memaco was designated sole and exclusive agent for all metals produced in Zambia, not only from existing mines but from future mines as well.

Obviously Memaco is now going through an extremely difficult period, primarily because of recession in the economic conditions of the world and the problems generated as a result. Memaco is also in the process of rationalising its activities and the service which was provided by the former companies. In the field of sub-agencies, the company will try whenever possible to market the copper direct and to resort to the employment of sub-agents only as a last measure. Even when sub-agencies are used, there will only be one sub-agent in each country as opposed to two and this will cut down on the duplication which was a feature of the previous arrangements. Memaco will, therefore, be saving a lot of valuable foreign exchange that previously used to go out in the form of commissions and fees. It is also hoped that because of one centralised marketing organisation, the availability of the Zambian brands, NCR, MCM, REC etc., will be more flexible as its intention is to give one contract for Zambian metals to various consumers.

The new marketing arrangements should be viewed as an

extension of government policy to expand its control of all vital and strategic industries in Zambia. It also gives an opportunity to the people of Zambia to be involved in the production, management and disposal of their valuable natural resources. These arrangements are not punitive and should not be seen as an affront to Anglo and Amax — indeed the retention of the 51 per cent in the mining and exploration of metals in Zambia is a clear indication of the amount of confidence the government has in these mining houses. Their role has been appreciated. Some form of Zambian participation in the mining industry was essential considering the importance of copper in the economy. It accounts for about 90 per cent of the domestic exports, 65 per cent of the foreign exchange earnings and is also responsible for about 16 per cent of total paid employment.

In these days of economic hardship every country has to tighten its belt and Zambia is no exception. The intention is that the outflow of foreign exchange which is vital for the development of the country should be controlled as stringently as possible and that all loopholes which existed in certain arrangements with big companies, private and state owned, have to be blocked. The role of the Central Bank and its commercial arm, the National Commercial Bank of Zambia Limited is extremely important in fulfilling the objectives of all these arrangements.

During the ten-year period of Zambian independence many attempts have been made to grapple with the problems of the mining industry. Current developments are not isolated from the mainstream of international affairs of our decade in both development and developed countries. All in all, the changes in Zambia are meant to lead to a greater prosperity for all and the beginning of economic independence.

13

Europe's Concessions to Africa — The ACP/EEC Negotiations

Many Arab leaders that I have spoken to do not want to duplicate other financial, technical and economic cooperation being given to the developing countries of Africa. They particularly wanted to know the nature of trade between African, Caribbean and Pacific (ACP) countries on the one hand and the European Economic Community (EEC) on the other. They were also interested in the financial and technical assistance the EEC is prepared to grant to ACP states.

Although this book is about the new economic and financial relationships between the Arab oil producing countries and the countries of Africa, it is useful to highlight the most important aspects of the new ACP/EEC Lome Convention, signed in February 1975. The Convention is unique in the sense that it has succeeded in bringing together three regions of the world into the ACP. That was the initial hurdle. The first official meeting between its member-states and the EEC states then took place in July and October 1973. At those meetings the ACP set out their policy objectives as follows:

a) negotiations should not result in a loss of any of the advantages, of whatever nature, enjoyed by the ACP states;

b) free and unlimited access for ACP products to the markets of EEC;

c) the fixing of the amount of aid from the Community to ACP states at a level which allows the real development needs of the ACP to be met;

d) unlike the Yaounde and East African Community (Arusha) Conventions, the advantages accorded to ACP by the Community should not be the subject of any reciprocity, account being taken of the difference in levels of development between ACP and the EEC.

Protracted discussions were undertaken in permanent

113

negotiating committee meetings in Brussels and at the joint Ministerial conferences in Kingston in July 1974, and in Brussels in January 1975. Although the provisions of the Convention are not as good as the ACP states would have liked them to be, the Convention as a whole is an improvement on both Yaounde and Arusha.

Shridath S. Ramphal, Guyana's Minister of Foreign Affairs, who ably represented not only his country but also the ACP in negotiating ACP/EEC trade cooperation said that the negotiations for the trade regime to be established under the Convention were difficult. It was essential that care be taken in the negotiations on the trade regime to ensure that the arrangements for trade cooperation under the new Convention do create a new and more satisfactory model of relationships between developed and developing countries.

It is fair to say that the character of the trade regime is very much consistent with the aspirations of the developing countries and provides a basis for further improvement. Under the present Convention ACP countries have gained the following:

a) Unlike the Yaounde and Arusha Conventions, the ACP/EEC Convention does not provide for reciprocity between developed and developing countries as a matter of contractual obligation. Although ACP countries have agreed to accord member-states of EEC no less favourable treatment than that accorded to third countries there is no obligation to give Europe more favoured treatment and especially no obligation to reciprocate by providing preferential access to ACP markets.

b) The provisions relating to establishments and payments and capital movements protect the basic position of the developing countries in that the repayment of capital in foreign exchange will be influenced by the economic position of the ACP state or states concerned.

c) The provisions for the stabilisation of export earnings introduce new arrangements which hold out a promise of contributing to a less insecure economic future for some ACP states.

d) The EEC have agreed to give access of 96 per cent to

ACP exportable agricultural products. It is true that this 96 per cent of ACP exportable agricultural products does not cover all products of ACP countries which earn foreign exchange. Those not covered can nevertheless be critical in the exports of particular ACP states. Despite this, the Convention must be seen as providing a potentiality for — but not an immediate guarantee of — access to the Community market. In order to accommodate products which are not included in the 96 per cent the ACP and EEC made a declaration to the effect that:

'The Community declares itself ready to begin an examination of requests by the ACP states that other agricultural products . . . should be made subject to special terms whether these are new agricultural products for which real possibilities for exporting to the EEC might exist or current products not covered by the present provisions in so far as these exports might assume an important position in the exports of one or more ACP states.'

The above formulation would have been better if it was drawn from Article 1 of the title which sets out the aims and objectives of the Convention and stresses the need for growth in ACP exports to the Community. However, the Community refused to go as far as that because in their opinion it would be unrealistic to use language in the declaration which implied commitment on access for the outstanding products. The present declaration is a reasonable compromise.

The critics of the Convention are likely to place emphasis on the following points:

a) The Community's unwillingness to increase the list of agricultural products covered by the Common Agricultural Policy for which it was willing to provide special measures for access will deprive some ACP states of market opportunities to which they had legitimately aspired.

b) The stabilisation of the export earnings scheme is materially limited in its immediate value to ACP states by the limitations on the range of exports covered, the threshold levels and the overall size of the fund.

c) Almost every beneficial arrangement authorised or
   assured by the Convention is hedged around by
   exceptions, qualifications and escape mechanisms
   operable for the greater part at the discretion of the
   EEC.

Despite the above handicaps and limitations, the Convention
has provided a model of new and satisfactory relationships. It is
a model which derives its real strength from its capacity for
growth: growth in such areas as enlargements of the list of
agricultural products liable to special treatment under the
Common Agricultural Policy provisions; growth in the list of
products to come under the stabilisation scheme; and above all
growth in the unity and solidarity of ACP states.

On 10 February 1975, ACP Ministers met in Accra to review
the final draft convention agreed upon by the bureau of the
ACP and EEC states in Brussels. In his opening address the
Ghanaian Head of State, Colonel I.K. Acheampong, expressed
some of the fears and anxieties shared not only by the ACP
states themselves but also by people who were not party to the
negotiations. There were fears that differences between the
various groups, the 'Associates', the 'Yaounde Group', the
'African Group' and the 'Commonwealth Group' might militate
against the supreme interest of the developing countries. There
were fears as to whether the EEC, with its large financial
resources, might try to bulldoze the financially weaker ACP
group. There were fears that the English and French languages
might operate as a barrier between Anglophone and
Francophone countries. On the other hand, the ACP states
realised their common needs, their common potential and
common destiny and worked together as a well-disciplined
team. Teamwork was even more important than the ability of
each country to negotiate on its own. The 'New Economic
Order', the most talked about expression at the UN, had now
been put into practice. A new economic relationship between
Europe and the countries of Africa, the Caribbean and the
Pacific, based on mutual trust and confidence, was being
established.

It falls outside the sphere of this book to deal with the
colonial history of ACP states and their new partners, the
member-states of the EEC, but I think it is quite appropriate to

state that European presence in Africa has always been motivated by commercial interests. Contrary to the views cherished by many historians and scholars, Europeans did not come to Africa solely to preach the gospel of God. They were attracted by gold, copper, diamonds, ivory, etc., and the fact that trade at that time was one-way traffic. In real terms there was nothing the African received for his gold, copper, ivory and sometimes his own being. The new economic arrangement between Europe and ACP states is at last a two-way traffic. Both partners will be able to balance their accounts without being forced to create suspense accounts for the missing items. Of course the developing countries must increase their productive capacity in order to benefit from the new economic order. Colonel Acheampong was expressing similar sentiments when he said: 'The recent history of the developing world of which we, the African, the Caribbean and Pacific countries form a vital part, has been marked by sustained effort to recapture the commanding heights of our economy and to acquire our just share of the proceeds of the world resources.'

Before the formal signing of the Convention in Lome, I had the opportunity to talk to President Kaunda of Zambia about his views on the Convention. The President said that if one was only concerned with the comparative benefits to member-states it is true that Zambia in the short run has the least benefits, but Zambia is an integral part of the ACP states and also, in the wider sense, of the developing countries. In his view, the ACP/EEC Lome Convention is an integral part of the process of redressing the world economic imbalance between the industrialised and the developing countries of the world. Some of the provisions of the Lome Convention are an improvement on what has been done by UNCTAD. President Kaunda, an advocate of the importance of man in society, was particularly happy with the new Convention in that the ACP states had throughout the negotiations protected the interests of the Group of seventy-seven (developing countries under UNCTAD). They resolved not to do anything which would be construed to be detrimental to the interest of other developing countries who are not party to this agreement.

President Kaunda considered the Lome Convention as a springboard for future trade among ACP states. Having concluded the new agreement with Europe, the ACP states should now use every ounce of energy towards the promotion of trade among themselves.

I asked the President whether there was any merit in signing the agreement if Zambia was apparently not going to benefit from the Convention. The President's reply was: 'Heat lost, heat gained.' He stressed the solidarity of the Third World. If it was true that ACP states as a group had gained then Zambia would be bound to benefit from closer economic cooperation either through the OAU or through the ACP states themselves.

Scholars and other pens more eloquent than mine will elaborate more on the shortcomings of the Lome Convention. But to all those people who wish to undertake this study in greater depth, I wish to suggest they take into account the following message from Colonel Acheampong:

> In recalling the difficulties you encountered and the reasons for these difficulties, your purpose would be not so much to assess the magnitude of what you did not obtain as to evaluate the extent to which you succeeded in eroding the interests and beliefs hitherto considered sacrosanct. Thus you may well feel that what is important is not that you did not obtain free access for all products falling under the Common Agricultural Policy, but that you were able to compel Europe to extend its initial offer to cover sensitive products like cut flowers, arrow roots and rice which had originally been excluded. And you may perhaps feel that, coupled with the commitment to engage in continuing dialogue on a case-by-case basis over the remaining products of actual or potential interest, it constitutes such a substantial compliance with our original principle of total free access as to engender a feeling of optimism.
>
> Thus, also, on rules of origin it is easy to feel disappointed at the limited success achieved. But it is also possible, having regard to the very nature of the problem and to the concessions obtained on cumulative origin, to regard this limited success as vindicating the principle you steadfastly maintained.

Mr Ramphal, Guyana's Foreign Minister, also had a word of

warning to ACP states. He cautioned them about being complacent about their relationship with Europe. He said:

> We must not mistake victory in the battle for an end to the war; and we must not win the war only to lose the peace. We must not rest upon the successes of the negotiations and ignore the essential need for continuing our strength in unity for a new international economic order within which our evolving relations with the European Community can find a propitious habitation. . . while the results of the negotiation are in many respects a valid cause for satisfaction, they do not in their totality constitute a fulfilment of the aspiration of the ACP states and it would be a dangerous pretence to believe otherwise.

It was clear from the Minister's message that it was unity more than any other factor that enabled ACP states to negotiate as a group and to arrive at a momentous decision to sign the Lome Agreement. The unity enabled ACP states not only to handle effectively the most sustained, the most purposeful and most effective negotiations ever conducted by the countries of the developing world with major industrial powers, but also to have an upper hand in the negotiations with the EEC. Mr Ramphal had this to say:

> The credit for that achievement is due in substantial measure to the solidarity which, to the consternation of our negotiating partners on the other side, grew stronger rather than weaker, grew more durable rather than more tenuous, with each passing month of the negotiations. There were times, indeed, when it was apparent to all of us that the unity of the Group of forty-six (ACP states) was more sturdy than that of the Community of nine (member states of EEC).

Apart from the writers and scholars, the criticism about the Lome Convention is likely to come from countries of the Third World who are not party to this convention and to the emerging countries of Africa and Asia. It is fair to say that the negotiators of the Lome Convention on both sides were constantly mindful of the obligations they owed to the developing countries of the world who were not represented at the negotiating table. Mr Ramphal was expressing the views of everybody who participated in the negotiations when he said:

> In terms of a wider search for consensus on the effective establishment of the New International Economic Order, we are convinced that in these negotiations we have protected those vital interests of the Third World and we are determined to ensure that in the implementation of the Convention we shall keep always in mind the reality that our relations with the EEC represent but a part of our relations with the rest of mankind. Whether in Europe or beyond, they are likewise only a part of the wider complex of relationships between the developed and the developing countries.

On 3-6 June 1975, the ACP Council of Ministers met in Georgetown, Guyana. At this meeting the council resolved to take the ACP group beyond the Lome Convention into the new era of intra-ACP partnership:
  a) Establishment of a register of exports available in the ACP states;
  b) Arrangements for exchange of information on approaches and techniques for development;
  c) Establishment of channels for disseminating news in place of the services now offered by metropolitan agencies;
  d) Promotion of economic cooperation including trade and transport expansion and joint industrial enterprises.

  The Prime Minister of Guyana, Mr Burnham, appealed to the delegates not to let the lure of short-term gain cause them to advance national interests at the expense of long-term unity and solidarity. The Prime Minister observed that it was natural for member-states of ACP to advance their individual national interest. This is natural because of their economic diversity and varying levels of development. Despite this hurdle, he appealed to the member-states that while not neglecting national objectives they should continue to remain united and together, sometimes sacrificing the individual short-term advantage for

HE Sir Seretse Khama, KBE MP
President of Republic of Botswana

HE Col Ignatius Kutu Acheampong
Head of State and Chairman of the Supreme Military Counsel

the long-term benefit of the group as a whole.

The main achievement of the ACP meeting in Georgetown was the adoption of a Georgetown Agreement institutionalising the group and taking the forty-six developing nations into a new era of economic cooperation. The ACP states agreed to take immediate steps to promote as much economic and other forms of cooperation among member-states as possible. They agreed to establish a number of working groups to conduct studies such as trade, industry, transport, communication and mobilisation of trained manpower. The conference also sought to allay the fears of other developing countries over the possible divisive potential of the Lome Convention, applied as it was to one group of the developing nations alone. They pledged to work together with other developing nations through international organisations such as UNCTAD.

The Council of Ministers expressed concern about the lack of consultation on the part of the Community in working out various regulations relating to the implementation of various protocols under the chapter dealing with General Trade Agreements. They went ahead to produce, for interim application, regulations relating to beef, veal and sugar without prior information or consultation with the ACP states. It is an open secret that the Community has laid down, for submission to the EEC Council of Ministers, draft regulations relating to the overall trade arrangements, rule of origin, common agricultural products, coal and steel and iron without informing or consulting the ACP. They regretted that the Convention had commenced on a very bad note.

When I checked this information with a senior official from the Community, he informed me that their rules of procedure do not allow any consultation on the draft regulations prior to the consent of member-states. He further pointed out that the Community wanted to avoid delays in establishing these regulations because of lack of time.

The Council noted that four ACP beef producing countries — Botswana, Kenya, Madagascar and Swaziland — had surplus beef supplies and were finding it difficult to gain access for it into the EEC markets. As a result of the restrictions and levies imposed by the Community, the beef and veal industry in some of the ACP states has deteriorated to the extent that in some

ACP states the industry is operating on a 25 per cent basis, while those still exporting to the Community market are losing thousands of dollars per month.

14
Important Provisions of the Lome Convention

Trade cooperation

ACP countries purchase consumer and capital goods from Europe. In an attempt to balance their balance of payments accounts, they have decided to encourage member-states of the Community to buy raw materials from ACP countries. The Charter of the Community does not permit membership of countries which have not yet attained economic development comparable to that of industrial countries of Europe. Hence ACP states do not qualify for membership. However, they can be accepted as associate members, and the ACP states have accepted associate membership of the EEC. The two parties have agreed to promote trade between them, with account being taken of their respective levels of development and in particular the Community must open its doors so that ACP states can sell their products in the Community market. The parties have agreed that it is the only way by which ACP states can accelerate the rate of their economic growth.

It has been agreed that certain products originating in the ACP states shall be imported into the Community duty-free of customs duties and of fiscal charges, levies and other charges having equivalent effect. The Community has stated that the products imported from ACP states will not be accorded treatment which will be more favourable than that accorded to products from member-states of the Community, because this would be tantamount to self-discrimination. It is important to note that the list of goods to be imported duty-free into the Community are mainly agricultural products which are not readily obtainable either within the Community or from their traditional sources.

The Community has agreed not to apply to imports of products originating in the ACP states any quantitative restrictions or measures having equivalent effect other than those which member-states apply among themselves. The parties are aware that they have no control over the situations of their respective economies and therefore if serious disturbances occur in a sector of the economy of a contracting state or if difficulties arise which result in a deterioration in the economic situation, the contracting state or states concerned may take the necessary protective measures; but these measures shall not exceed the limit of what is strictly necessary to remedy the difficulties that have arisen.

It is now fashionable for most trade agreements to include the most favoured nation clause. The convention between ACP states and the Community is no exception. The most favoured nation clause presented great difficulties and was not settled until the last moment. Essentially, the problem was in respect of the Community's proposal that the most favoured nation treatment should apply to ACP exports in their widest sense. According to the Community's viewpoint, the most favoured nation treatment would apply not merely to imports and exports, but also to exports as such — that it would represent a guarantee of the supply of raw materials.

The ACP countries were prepared to grant the Community most favoured nation treatment in terms of Article 1(i) of the GATT, which limited the most favoured nation treatment to import and export duties and related administrative procedures. The same treatment would be extended to the Community's economic operators, nationals, firms and companies and ACP countries shall see to it that their public bodies do likewise.

Obviously it is not difficult to understand why the Community would like the ACP countries to offer the most favoured nation treatment to the Community in respect of both imports and exports. They are concerned about the mineral exports of ACP countries. Zambia's copper, for example, is considered to be of a very good quality and therefore they would like a good share of mineral exports from Africa. This appears to be a one-way traffic because when ACP countries ask for similar treatment the member-states of the Community are reluctant to grant it on the ground that their internal laws do not permit them to sell certain goods and services for strategic reasons. They also say that they run free economies and therefore they are not in a position to take necessary steps to ensure that their public bodies, economic operators and nationals offer the most favoured nation treatment to ACP states. It is extremely difficult for the developing countries to give unconditional most favoured nation treatment to industrial countries, i.e. if a third party wants to construct a railway line between two ACP states and that third party is prepared to offer a loan interest-free, the member-state or states of the community who want to obtain this contract cannot solely rely on the most favoured nation treatment. The member-state or states should be able to meet the same conditions, namely to provide finance interest-free. Anything short of this would be construed as naked exploitation of developing countries.

The EEC wishes to have a specific assurance of the most favoured nation treatment in terms not only of Article 1(i) of the GATT, but of Article XIII as well, which deals with quantitative restrictions. The formulation which now appears in the agreement was a compromise by the two parties. It makes no reference to the GATT. It is simply an undertaking by ACP not to discriminate against the EEC member-states. It does not constitute an unqualified guarantee of exports to member-states of the Community.

Another objectionable clause in the Convention is that relating to the communication of information of the budget proposals of a contracting state. For example, when a country like Jamaica wants to impose customs duty on spaghetti they should, prior to taking such a decision, inform Italy and obtain her reaction. Apart from the fact that such a procedure would create a lot of administrative problems, it would also amount to releasing the budget proposal to an outsider before national Parliaments have had the opportunity to look at it. There is no guarantee that these proposals would not fall into the hands of some unscrupulous operators who would like to benefit at the expense of ACP states.

The Community had submitted that there should be general provisions for consultation in the field of trade cooperation. They said that during the duration of the Convention, ACP states and the Community should adopt a joint declaration concerning the presentation of their viewpoints to GATT. The ACP insisted that any obligation to consult with the

Community should be strictly limited to the implementation of the provisions of the Convention and should not cover the entire field of international trade. By virtue of their differences in economic development, their interests are bound to differ and therefore each party will have to ensure that their interests are protected. The strength of the present Convention lies in the fact that ACP states have striven to protect the interest of other developing countries who are not party to this Convention. They refused to accept a consultation machinery which was likely to impair the solidarity of the Third World at international forums.

The Convention recognised that most of the economic operators of the Community are not aware of raw materials produced by ACP states. It has therefore been agreed that the contracting parties shall carry out trade promotion activities. These activities will include:

i) improving the structure, the working methods of organisation of departments or firms contributing to the development of the foreign trade of ACP states or setting up such organisations, departments or firms;

ii) basic training or advanced vocational training of staff in trade promotion;

iii) participation by the ACP states in fairs, exhibitions, specialised international shows and the organisation of trade events;

iv) improving cooperation between economic operators in the EEC and the ACP states and establishing links to promote such cooperation;

v) carrying out and making use of market research and marketing studies;

vi) producing and distributing trade information in various forms within the Community and the ACP states with a view to developing trade.

It is fair to say that only the least developed countries of ACP are likely to derive maximum benefit from their association with the Community. The Community would like to maintain their traditional trade patterns. They are only prepared to buy from ACP countries the raw materials which their traditional sources are unable to supply.

It is generally believed that ACP states of the British

Commonwealth have benefited more from the UK market than they will from the enlarged Community. The UK market, though limited, absorbed all products coming from the Commonwealth countries free of duties and other charges. It will be difficult to exploit the larger market in the face of the barriers erected to protect this market. It is difficult to see how a country like Botswana can benefit from the enlarged Community if she is not allowed to sell all her beef to the Community. In determining the price for products from ACP countries the Community would like to pay little attention to the cost of production of a given commodity. For example, the Community would like to equate the price of sugar made of sugar cane to that made of sugar beet and yet the costs of production are different. It costs more to produce sugar from sugar cane than from sugar beet.

Semi-finished and finished products from ACP countries are subjected to such high tariffs that it is correct to classify them as prohibited goods. With this prohibitive rate of tariffs, the so-called trade cooperation between ACP states and the Community is nothing more than an academic exercise. On the one hand, they are telling the ACP countries to acquire sufficient technical know-how in order to progress from the stage of being merely producers of raw materials to the stage of processing their raw materials into semi-finished and finished products, and on the other hand they are unwilling to admit into their enlarged market semi-finished and finished products from ACP countries.

Financial and technical cooperation

The Convention on Financial and Technical Cooperation provides that the purpose of economic, financial and technical cooperation is to correct the structural imbalances in the various sectors of the ACP countries' economies. It shall relate to the execution of projects and programmes which contribute essentially to the economic and social development of those countries. The cooperation shall complement the efforts of the ACP countries. In other words, the ACP countries concerned must be seen to be making efforts to improve the situation of their economy.

The Community would like to be assured that the funds it

will provide will be spent on projects which will benefit a large section of the population. To this end, the Convention provides that the relevant institutions of both the EEC and ACP countries concerned shall review at least once a year the work done under financial and technical cooperation. They shall take stock, on the basis of information gathered by both parties. The Community undertakes to provide ACP countries with an annual report on the management of the Community's financial and technical aid. The report will, in particular, show the position as to the commitment, implementation and utilisation of the aid and the countries which have benefited from it. The ACP countries undertake to inform the Community of any comments or proposals on the problems pertaining to the implementation in each ACP country of the economic, financial and technical cooperation. After the Community and ACP countries have compared their notes, they will jointly formulate resolutions on the measures to be undertaken in order to ensure that the objectives of such cooperation are attained.

The source of finance for the cooperation will be the European Development Fund and the European Investment Bank. Finance from the European Development Fund will be in the form of a grant, special loans and risk capital. The Bank will give loans on a concessionary rate of interest. The rate of interest shall be the rate charged by the Bank at the time of signature of each loan contract. The rate shall generally be reduced by 3 per cent by means of an interest rate subsidy, except where the loans are intended for investment in the oil sector, wherever they are located, or in the mining sector, unless in the latter case they are located in one of the least developed states. The Community's aid shall be 3,390 million units of account. This amount includes:

1. 3,000 million units of account from the European Development Fund allocated as follows:
   (a) for the purposes set out in Article I of Financial and Technical Cooperation:
   2,625 million units of account, consisting of:
   — 2,100 million units of account in the form of grants;
   — 430 million units of account in the form of special loans;
   — 95 million units of account in the form of risk capital.

(b) 375 million units of account has been earmarked for the purpose of stabilisation of export earnings.

2. For the purposes set out in Article I of Financial and Technical Cooperation, 390 million units of account shall be in the form of loans from the Bank.

The Community and the ACP state or states concerned will jointly decide whether a given project will be financed through the Bank or the Fund. The decision in each case will be influenced by the level of development and the economic and financial situation of the ACP state or states concerned. In other words, the ability to pay principal will apply. They will also take into account the nature of the project or programme and financial profitability and of its economic and social impact. For example, productive capital projects in the industrial, tourism and mining sectors will be financed by means of loans from the Bank and risk capital.

Money from both the Bank and the Fund will be used to finance the following projects and programmes:

i) schemes to improve the structure of agricultural production;

ii) capital projects in the fields of rural development, industrialisation, energy, mining, tourism and economic social infrastructure;

iii) industrial information and promotion schemes;

iv) marketing and sales promotion schemes;

v) specific schemes to help small- and medium-sized national firms;

vi) micro-projects for grassroots development, in particular in rural areas.

Since the assistance from the Community is supposed to supplement the efforts of the ACP states, the financial and technical cooperation shall not cover current administrative, maintenance and operating expenses; but will cover local and import costs connected with the projects and programmes being carried out by the Community in any ACP countries.

The Community recognises that ACP countries have reached different levels of economic development and therefore it is necessary to offer them different types of assistance. In the implementation of financial and technical cooperation the least developed states will receive preferential treatment so as to reduce specific obstacles which impede their development and prevent them from taking full advantage of the opportunities offered by financial and technical cooperation. At the time when the Convention came into force, the following countries were eligible for preferential treatment: Botswana, Burundi, Central African Republic, Mauritania, Niger, Rwanda, Somalia, Sudan, Swaziland, Tanzania, Togo, Tonga, Upper Volta, Western Samoa. Any country of ACP which is not included in this list would qualify if its economic situation undergoes a radical and lasting change so as to necessitate preferential treatment. A country may also be dropped from the list if its economic position improves to the extent that special treatment is no longer warranted.

In general, all ACP states are eligible for financial and technical cooperation. The assistance is extended to:

a) regional bodies to which the ACP states belong and which are authorised by them;

b) the joint bodies set up by the ACP states to achieve certain specific objectives;

c) local authorities and public or semi-public development agencies of the ACP states, in particular their development banks;

d) private bodies working in the countries concerned for the economic and social development of the population of those countries;

e) firms carrying on their activities in accordance with the methods of industrial and business management and which are set up as companies or firms of an ACP state;

f) groups of producers that are nationals of the ACP states or like bodies, and, where no such groups or bodies exist, the producers themselves;

g) for training purposes, scholarship and trainees.

In the case of ACP countries which have development plans, the Community's aid shall be integrated in those plans so that projects undertaken with the financial assistance of the Community dovetail with the objectives and priorities set by those states. Since development plans in the developing countries are very much influenced by the economic and monetary situations in the industrial countries the Community has agreed to make its aid flexible in order to accommodate economic and monetary changes both in the industrial and developing countries. The Community will not finance projects in any ACP country or countries unless it is satisfied that the projects or programmes stem from economic or social development plans of the ACP states. There should be proper appraisal of the project to ensure that in each project expected effects are the practical expression of a number of specific development objectives of the state or states concerned. The appraisal shall ensure that as far as possible the schemes selected constitute the most effective and profitable method of achieving their objective, and it will be done jointly by the Community and the ACP states and any other beneficiaries.

The ACP states would like most of the projects to be undertaken by the Community in ACP countries to be carried out by national firms. By so doing they will be in a position to kill two birds with one stone. They will generate employment within the country or countries concerned and will also be in a position to earn foreign exchange which may later be used to repay the loan used to finance the project. When a national firm has used all local expenditure it will be paid in local currency whereas a firm which is neither a national or resident in the ACP state will remit all its earnings to overseas countries, sometimes without even paying income tax. Most double taxation conventions which have been concluded in the last five years are based on the OECD draft which provides that any person, firm, corporation or individual who is resident in a contracting state will not be liable to tax in other contracting states for a period not exceeding six months. Often foreign firms arrange their affairs in such a way that their businesses are concluded within six months. They have no permanent establishment as defined in the OECD and therefore they skilfully avoid tax.

The Community, on the other hand, would like firms belonging to member-states to participate in the projects of ACP states which are financed through the Fund or Bank. There is, therefore, a conflict of interest. As a compromise, it has been agreed that in general operations financed by the Community contracts will go to open tender. The award of contracts shall be open on equal terms to all natural and legal persons of the member-states and the ACP states. The

Community and ACP states should adhere to the following procedure:

i) ensure advance publication in reasonable time of invitations to tender in the official journals of the European
Community and the official journals of the ACP states;

ii) eliminate any discriminatory practice or technical specification liable to stand in the way of participation on equal
terms by all natural or legal persons of the member-states
and ACP states;

iii) encourage in so far as possible, especially where major
works or those of a particularly technical nature are to be
undertaken, cooperation between the firms of the member-
states and of the ACP states, for example by means of pre-
selection and the creation of groups.

The Community did, however, recognise the fact that there
may be cases in which it would not be economically
advantageous to companies of member-states to participate in
the tender. There can be cases in which the works to be
undertaken, because of their scale, would only interest local
firms of ACP states. In those exceptional cases it has been
agreed to use an accelerated procedure for issuing invitations to
tender, involving a shorter time limit for the submission of
tenders. This accelerated procedure will be restricted to tenders
whose value is estimated at less than 2,000,000 units of
account. It shall be used only for works contracts and in any
case the tender will comply with the rules in force in the ACP
state concerned.

The ACP states have stated that they are not only interested
in setting up industries but they are also interested in providing
employment for their nationals during the course of
construction of a given project. In view of this it has been
agreed that where two tenders are acknowledged to be
equivalent in respect of qualifications and guarantees and
above all the price, preference shall be given to the one which
permits labour intensive methods of ACP countries.

The tender procedures are very much similar to those of the
World Bank. They are designed in such a way that contracts
will invariably be awarded to firms of industrial contracts.
Although in theory the Community and ACP countries will be
required to take the necessary implementing measures to

ensure equality of conditions for participation in tendering procedures for the award of contracts, the Community, by virtue of being the donor, will ensure that their views prevail on who should be awarded the contract. After all, most ACP countries will not possess the technical know-how and therefore most of the appraisals for ACP contracts will be done by agents appointed by the Community, who invariably will have vested interests in various companies domiciled in member-states.

In some African countries some foreign companies have created a monopoly in winning government contracts because they have planted their men in government departments charged with the responsibility of appraising contracts which go to open tender. They know the estimated price and therefore it is quite possible for them to provide calculations which correspond fairly with the estimated contract price.

The Convention on Financial and Technical Cooperation between the EEC and the ACP states is very similar to the Yaounde Convention. The Yaounde Convention was exploited by some member-states of the Community, France being the main culprit. The so-called national farms in former French colonies are owned and controlled by French nationals. When the Community offered financial assistance to their French colonies to develop their farming industry, the money found its way into the pockets of French entrepreneurs operating in former French colonies. It was in a way a direct subsidy to the French economy. One hopes that the same mistake will not be repeated.

Current payments and movements of capital

In order to protect their investments in ACP countries, the Community have stated that ACP countries should undertake to do the following things:

  i) should not discriminate among nationals, companies or firms of member-states of EEC in respect of such arrangements as may be applied in matters of establishment and provision of services;
  ii) should one or more ACP state grant nationals or companies of a third state more favourable treatment as regards establishment or provision of services such treatment should also be accorded to member-states of EEC;

iii) with regard to capital movement linked with investments and to current payments the ACP countries should refrain from taking such action in the foreign exchange area which would amount to discrimination against companies or firms of the member-states of EEC;

iv) to accord nationals and companies or firms of the member-states treatment at least equal to that which they accord to the most favoured third states;

v) to make available to companies or firms of EEC the currency necessary for the payment of interest and commission on and amortisation of loans and capital aid granted for the implementation of aid measures on their territory;

vi) to make available to the European Investment Bank the foreign exchange necessary for the transfer of all sums received by it in national currency which represent the net revenue and proceeds from transactions involving participation by the Community.

In practice ACP states will find it difficult to comply with the conditions imposed by the Community. As stated earlier in the section dealing with trade promotion, the EEC member-states should meet the same conditions granted to the non-member-states if they want the most favoured nation treatment to be granted to them. The Community demands that ACP states should accord nationals and companies or firms of ACP states treatment at least equal to that which they accord to the most favoured third state. This clause requires proper balance. It is only fair and proper that the obligations should be on both contracting parties and not only on the ACP states. In other words the arrangements should be reciprocal.

The will to meet their contractual obligations is there, but ACP states may not have the means at a given time to extinguish their indebtedness. There must be exceptions for reasons of serious economic disturbances or balance of payments problems. It must also be appreciated that ACP states have embarked on various development programmes aimed at improving the standard of living of the masses of their people. In order to contain the cash flow problems their foreign exchange regulations provide that foreign firms operating in their countries should plough back into the country some of the profits earned; Ghana is a notable example. The Community is saying that such companies should be allowed to repatriate all their net profits.

Export earnings from commodities

The Community has agreed to devise a system which will remedy the harmful effects of the instability of export earnings of ACP countries. This system is supposed to ensure sustained growth of the economies of ACP countries. The main tenet of the system is to stabilise earnings from exports by ACP to the Community of certain products on which their economies are dependent and which are affected by the fluctuations in price or quantity or both.

The two parties have agreed that export earnings to which the stabilisation system will apply shall be those accruing from export by ACP countries to the Community of the products agreed upon. The object of the exercise will be to improve employment opportunities in ACP countries and the terms of trade between the ACP state concerned and the Community. The Community will pay particular attention to least developed states, landlocked and island ACP states.

The following products shall be included in the commodities for export earnings:
 a) *Groundnut Products*
    groundnuts, shelled or not
    groundnut oil
    groundnut oilcake
 b) *Cocoa Products*
    cocoa beans
    cocoa paste
    cocoa butter
 c) *Coffee Products*
    raw or roasted coffee
    coffee extracts or essences
 d) *Cotton Products*
    cotton, not carded or combed
    cotton lint
    coton waste, not carded or combed
    cotton carded or combed
 e) *Coconut Products*
    coconuts

      copra
      coconut oil
      coconut oil cake

f) *Palm, Palm Nut and Kernel Products*
      palm oil
      palm nut and kernel
      palm nut and kernel oil
      palm nut and kernel oilcake

g) *Raw Hides, Skins and Leather*
      raw hides and skins
      bovine cattle leather
      sheep and lamb skin leather
      goat and kid skin leather

h) *Wood Products*
      wood in the rough
      wood roughly squared or half squared, but not further manufactured
      wood sawn lengthwise, but not further manufactured
      plywood, blockboard, laminboard, battenboard and similar laminated wood products.

i) *Fresh Bananas*

j) *Tea*

k) *Raw Sisal*

l) *Iron Ore*
      iron ores and concentrates and roasted iron pyrites

The ACP states have not been happy with the EEC offer in respect of commodities which come under the EEC Common Agricultural Policy (CAP). The EEC tended to place low priority on the negotiations on CAP products. The ACP countries attached great importance to trade in agricultural products because the economies of some of the ACP states depend to a very large extent on agriculture. The EEC contended that the list offered to ACP for the agricultural products to enter duty-free in the enlarged EEC market accounts for 96 per cent of ACP agricultural produce. Only 4 per cent of ACP products will be subject to CAP regulations. The ACP states argued that some of their member-states rely for almost all their export earnings on the products which have not been granted free access.

It has been agreed that the statistics used for

HE Jaalle Major General Mohamed Siad Barre
President Somali Democratic Republic

HE Lt Gen Mobutu Sese Seko
President of Republic of Zaire

implementation of the system shall be those obtained by crosschecking the statistics of the ACP states and of the EEC, account being taken of the f.o.b. values.

The system shall be restricted to products listed above where they are: (a) released from home use in the Community; (b) brought under the inward processing traffic system there in order to be processed. The stabilisation of export earnings proposed by the Community is very discriminatory. One of the main features of the system is that it shall apply to an ACP state's export earnings from the product listed above if, during the year preceding the year of application, earnings from export of the product or products to all destinations represented at least 10 per cent of its total earnings from merchandise exports; for sisal, however, the percentage shall be 5 per cent. In the case of least developed, landlocked and island ACP states this percentage shall be reduced to 2.5 per cent. The Community has emphasised that the system shall apply to export earnings from a list of products which are essentially important because of the place they occupy in the economy.

The system is very flexible. It provides that if, after twenty-four months from the date the Convention comes into force, one or more products not contained in the said list which constitute an essential product upon which one or more ACP countries depend to a very large extent are affected by sharp fluctuations, the Community will give sympathetic consideration to the product or products to be included in the list. To avoid smuggling and trafficking in products from non-ACP countries, ACP states concerned shall certify that the products to which the stabilisation system applies have originated in their territory.

Appendix

——————————————————————————

Statistical Data Relating to Aid from the Arab States and Iran to African and Other Countries

1. Bilateral aid from Arab States and Iran to the developing countries of Africa, if possible up to the end of March 1975, broken down in the following ways: (a) by donors and recipients; (b) by commitments and actual disbursements.

2. Multilateral aid from Arab States and Iran through agencies such as the Arab Bank for Africa, the Special Arab Fund for Africa, the Arab-African Bank, the Islamic Development Bank and the Arab Technical Assistance Fund for Africa, etc., if possible listing the size of allocations to each recipient.

3. Multilateral aid from Arab States and Iran through international agencies such as the UN Special Emergency Fund.

1. (a) Bilateral Aid Commitments from Arab to African (Non-Arab)* States, 1974 (US $ millions)

RECIPIENTS	Algeria	Iran	Iraq	Kuwait	Libya	Qatar	Saudi Arabia	UAE	TOTAL
Burundi					1.0				1.0
Chad				8.3	7.6	1.9			17.8
Dahomey									0.0
Equat. Guinea				15.0	1.0				16.0
Ethiopia					1.0				1.0
Gambia					1.4				1.4
Guinea					10.1				10.1
Lesotho		1.0			0.5				1.5
Mali	1.2								1.2
Mauritania			2.5	3.3	5.1	9.9	35.2	15.0	71.0
Niger									0.0
Sahel region								6.0	6.0
Senegal		10.7							10.7
Somalia			17.5	7.0	9.6	14.0	30.0	19.5	97.6
Sudan		64.0	10.0	15.6		14.0	14.4	21.1	139.1
Togo					1.2				1.2
Uganda					14.9				14.9
Upper Volta					0.7				0.7
Zaire								26.0	26.0
Zambia	0.8								0.8
TOTALS	2.0	75.7	30.0	48.9	54.1	39.7	80.0	87.6	418.0

1. (b) Bilateral Aid Disbursements from Arab to African States, 1974

It is not yet possible to provide a detailed breakdown by donor and recipient; in any case there is some artificiality in this concept, as the overall aid commitments of Arab states increased so greatly in 1974 that two factors would tend to give a misleadingly low figure for actual disbursements: (a) the time lag between commitment and disbursement; (b) the fact that some commitments are anyway spread over some years. However, the following estimates of actual receipts of aid may be useful:

Guinea: 5 million dollars
Senegal: 5 million dollars
Somalia: 25 million dollars
Sudan: 70 million dollars
Uganda: 2 million dollars
Mauritania: 25 million dollars
Other African states: 46 million dollars

Total: 178 million dollars

2. Multilateral Aid for Africa, 1974 and early 1975

Special Arab Fund for Africa. Created by Arab oil producers in January 1974 (i.e. excluding Iran). Allocations of original $200 million decided by OAU in August 1974. Disbursement started in October. Following figures give commitments from August 1974, together with estimated disbursements to March 1975.

1. (Most Seriously Affected countries — resulting from oil price rise) — 'MSA Group'.

	Commitments	*Disbursements*
	($ millions)	
Ethiopia	14.2	14.2
Tanzania	14.2	7.1
Sudan	10.6	5.3
Chad	8.8	8.8
Ghana	8.8	4.4
Mali	7.8	3.9
Senegal	7.5	7.5
Ivory Coast	7.2	3.6
Cameroon	5.7	2.85
Niger	5.4	2.7
Upper Volta	5.4	2.7
Malagasy Republic	4.8	2.4
Sierra Leone	3.6	1.8
Kenya	3.6	3.6
Lesotho	2.8	1.4
Dahomey	2.4	1.2
Central African Republic	2.4	2.4
Mauritania	2.1	1.05
Somalia	2.0	1.0
Guinea	1.6	0.8
Total	120.9	78.7

2. Other countries.

	Commitments	Disbursements
	($ millions)	
Zambia	12.7	12.7
Zaire	12.4	—
Morocco	11.8	5.9
Uganda	11.3	11.3
Malawi	7.5	—
Botswana	5.4	5.4
Swaziland	4.2	2.1
Liberia	3.6	1.8
Mauritius	2.7	2.7
Burundi	2.0	1.0
Rwanda	2.0	2.0
Togo	1.8	0.9
Gambia	0.7	0.35
Guinea-Bissau	0.5	0.5
Equat. Guinea	0.5	0.5
Total for 'other countries'	79.1	47.15
Combined Total MSA plus other countries	200.0	125.85

Arab Bank for Economic Development in Africa. Creation of this bank was originally agreed at sixth Arab summit meeting in Algeria in November 1973, and effectively started work at its Khartoum headquarters in January 1975. ABEDA will administer the Special Fund for Africa. In addition it has a capital of 231 million dollars, of which 33.4 million had been actually paid in by March 1975:

Saudi Arabia: 12.5 million dollars
Algeria: 5 million dollars
Kuwait: 5 million dollars
Qatar: 5 million dollars
Morocco: 2.9 million dollars
Tunisia: 1.25 million dollars
Oman: 1 million dollars
Bahrain: 0.25 million dollars
Jordan: 0.25 million dollars
Sudan: 0.25 million dollars

Arab African Bank. Established in 1964; by early 1974 it had provided loans totalling 18 million dollars to African states; in August its capital was increased to 50 million dollars. This money does not appear to have been committed to specific countries by early 1975.

3. **Commitments and Disbursements to United Nations Development Work 1974 (US $ millions)**

Donor	UN Agencies	UN Emergency Operation	Intnl. Develpmt. Assn.	Total
Algeria				
committed	0.5	20		20.5
disbursed	0.5	10		10.5
Iran				
committed	2.4	20		22.4
disbursed	2.4	20		22.4
Iraq				
committed	0.5			0.5
disbursed	0.5			0.5
Kuwait				
committed	0.6		32.0	32.6
disbursed	0.6		10.7	11.3
Libya				
committed	0.7			0.7
disbursed	0.7			0.7
Qatar				
committed	0.2			0.2
disbursed	0.2			0.2
Saudi Arabia				
committed	13.4	30		43.4
disbursed	13.4	30		43.4
UAE				
committed	0.5	10		10.5
disbursed	0.5	10		10.5
Total				
committed	18.8	80	32.0	130.8
disbursed	18.8	70	10.7	99.5

Source: Middle East Economic Consultants

Index

For Product Safety Concerns and Information please contact our EU
representative GPSR@taylorandfrancis.com
Taylor & Francis Verlag GmbH, Kaufingerstraße 24, 80331 München, Germany